# The Exodus Story

## ANCIENT
## AND MODERN
## PARALLELS

# ANCIENT
# AND MODERN
# PARALLELS

Richard Neitzel Holzapfel

BOOKCRAFT
Salt Lake City, Utah

Library of Congress Catalog Card Number: 97-76973
ISBN 1-57008-338-X


First Printing, 1997


Printed in the United States of America

For
Ed Griffith, Tom Murray, Von Packard, and Jack Rushton

*And behold, all things have their likeness, and all things are created and made to bear record of me, both things which are temporal, and things which are spiritual; things which are in the heavens above, and things which are on the earth, and things which are in the earth, and things which are under the earth, both above and beneath: all things bear record of me.*

—MOSES 6:63

c‑ɔ

*We were Pharaoh's bondmen in Egypt; and the Lord brought us out of Egypt with a mighty hand: and the Lord shewed signs and wonders, great and sore, upon Egypt, upon Pharaoh, and upon all his household, before our eyes: and he brought us out from thence, that he might bring us in, to give us the land which he sware unto our fathers. And the Lord commanded us to do all these statutes, to fear the Lord our God, for our good always, that he might preserve us alive.*

—DEUTERONOMY 6:21–24

c‑ɔ

*I did liken all scriptures unto us, that it might be for our profit and learning.*

—1 NEPHI 19:23

c‑ɔ

*A brief overview of the "plan of happiness" (which is my choice, my favorite title, in talking of the plan), if given at the very beginning and revisited occasionally, will be of immense value to your students. . . . You will not be with your students or your own children at the time of their temptations. At those dangerous moments they must depend on their own resources. If they can locate themselves within the framework of the gospel plan, they will be immensely strengthened. The plan is worthy of repetition over and over again. Then the purpose of life, the reality of the Redeemer, and the reason for the commandments will stay with them. Their gospel study, their life experiences, will add to an ever-growing witness of the Christ, of the Atonement, of the restoration of the gospel.*

—ELDER BOYD K. PACKER,
BYU SYMPOSIUM, 10 AUGUST 1993

# Contents

# Acknowledgments

The efforts of my publisher, Bookcraft, Inc., especially Cory Maxwell, Jana Erickson, and Gary Garff, are greatly appreciated. Hugh Nibley showed how the book of Exodus was a "type and a shadow of things" in an undergraduate class during my studies at BYU in the 1975–76 academic year. Jeff Cottle and Jeni Broberg Holzapfel provided comments, suggestions, insights, and critique on presentations that incorporated Hugh Nibley's insights over many years, beginning with my first presentation on this topic in 1978. S. Kent Brown, a former graduate professor of mine and now a colleague and mentor, was kind enough to share insights from his work on the Exodus pattern during my research on the subject. Finally, I am grateful to the Instructional Design Division (presently known as the Materials Management Division) of the LDS Church Educational System for preparing the illustrations included in this book as slides for a presentation on this topic titled "Temple Worship in the Old Testament," given at the 1987 Annual Scripture Symposium at Brigham Young University.

# Introduction

The Lord commanded the children of Israel in the book of Deuteronomy: "Remember that thou wast a servant in the land of Egypt, and that the Lord thy God brought thee out thence through a mighty hand and by a stretched out arm" (Deuteronomy 5:15). One of the most important words in any language is *remember.*

In Deuteronomy the divine call to remember is a common theme. It is summarized in the phrase "Remember the days of old" (Deuteronomy 32:7). Called the Deuteronomic imperative, the summon to remember could be appropriately identified as the eleventh commandment.[1] The Latter-day Saints, as part of the sacramental covenant, partake of the bread each Sabbath. The prayer states in part: "Bless and sanctify this bread to the souls of all those who partake of it, that they may eat in remembrance of the body of thy Son . . . and always remember him" (D&C 20:77). Likewise, the prayer for the water states: "Bless and sanctify this [water] to the souls of all those who drink of it, that they may do it in remembrance of the blood of thy Son, . . . that they do always remember him" (D&C 20:79). While remembering the past is important, the scriptures teach that not all of the past is worthy of recording or remembering. The scriptures remind us that it is the mighty works of God that are to be remembered and celebrated and that are of particular importance, especially the stories of how God delivered his covenant people.

Of all the stories of deliverance in the Old Testament, none remotely compares with the drama of the Exodus story as described in the second book of the Pentateuch (five books of Moses), named in Hebrew after the first two words, *we'elleh shemoth* ("these are the names of").² To most of us, it is known as Exodus, a Latin word derived from the Greek *Exodos,* a word which means "departure."³

While it is certainly a literary masterpiece in the way it maintains the expectations of the reader and brings the narrative to the climax of the tenth plague of the death of the firstborn, it is also important because it reveals in a fundamental way how God remembers his people and how he prepares a way for their deliverance. In one of the fullest and richest narratives found in scripture, the Lord demonstrates how he raised up a mediator, Moses, to deliver the children of Israel from Pharaoh's bitter bondage and established his earthly kingdom among them by making a covenant with them and finally establishing his tabernacle, the sign of his presence, in their midst. Moses, Joshua, and other prophets, including Nephi and Joseph Smith, appealed to the Exodus story as the most decisive proofs of God's mercy, goodness and power.⁴ Such is the story—a story that demonstrates the Lord's divine purpose, which is ultimately fulfilled through Christ Jesus our Redeemer.

The Lord often commanded ancient Israel: "Thou shalt remember that thou wast a bondman in Egypt, and the Lord thy God redeemed thee thence" (Deuteronomy 24:18). Moses himself said, "O Lord God, thou hast begun to shew thy servant thy greatness, and thy mighty hand: for what God is there in heaven or in earth, that can do according to thy works, and according to thy might?" (Deuteronomy 3:24.) Additionally, Moses reflected: For what God has taken him "a nation from the midst of another nation, . . . by signs, and by wonders, and by war, and by a mighty hand, and by a stretched out arm, and by great terrors?" (Deuteronomy 4:34.)

The Exodus story reminds us that the Lord delivers his covenant sons and daughters from temporal captivity from time to time to not only relieve suffering but to remind them that it is his ultimate purpose to deliver them from spiritual captivity.⁵ The story of the Lord's power to deliver is told over and over again in scripture, both modern and ancient. In certain places those scriptures show parallels between the ancient exodus and other moments in history and heighten our appreciation for God's power, mercy, and goodness.

These parallels, often identified as typologies, represent the interconnection between past, present, and future. Sometimes ancient events are but a foreshadowing of some future event. In the book of Moses, the Lord said: "And behold, all things have their likeness, and all things are created and made to bear record of me, both things which are temporal, and things which are spiritual; things which are in the heavens above, and things which are on the earth, and things which are in the earth, and things which are under the earth, both above and beneath: all things bear record of me" (Moses 6:63).

In a sense, then, the Old Testament prepares the world for the coming of Jesus Christ by bearing record of his life, ministry, death, and resurrection as it tells its stories and records its prophecies. Additionally, the stories of the ancient men and women in the Old Testament can be applied to our own lives, giving us examples to live by or examples to warn us. Finding these prophecies, parallels, and modern applications are some of the important reasons for studying the Old Testament.⁶

There is a caution, however. The Book of Mormon prophet Jacob warned that it is possible to seek for "things that [we cannot] understand" (Jacob 4:14), with the result of becoming blind to the spiritual reality of the scriptures. Jacob further taught that this blindness is a result of "looking beyond the mark" (Jacob 4:14). Looking beyond the mark, at least in one setting, may mean looking for parallels that do not exist, trying to make too much of things, or seeing some symbolic meaning in every action, object, and event. The natural result of looking beyond the mark is destruction, "for God hath taken away his plainness from them, and delivered unto them many things which they cannot understand, because they desired it. And because they desired it God hath done it, that they may stumble." (Jacob 4:14.)

As my university students remind me from time to time, I often repeat a phrase during the semester: "Analogies and parallels always break down." Parallels and analogies are often just a means to help one to understand or reinforce a concept. Trying to push them beyond a reasonable interpretation can be a way of missing the point. Additionally, sometimes a parallel may not have been originally intended by the author, and only after subsequent events have transpired can one see a parallel. Finally, some authors employed the Exodus pattern as an application in order to emphasize their purpose. In this light, the Exodus story provides a way to see the past and link it with the present.

This essay is intended for the lay member of the Church and not for my university colleagues. It is, therefore, an effort to expand the walls of my undergraduate classroom to include a much larger group of students who are not familiar with the scholarly literature and current research on this topic. Additionally, this effort is more of an application in the spirit of Nephi's direction found in 1 Nephi 19:23 than an exegetical treatment of the study. Without trying to look beyond the mark and with the stipulation that all parallels and analogies break down, let us begin to examine a story that will help us "remember that thou wast a servant in the land of Egypt, and that the Lord thy God brought thee out thence through a mighty hand and by a stretched out arm" (Deuteronomy 5:15).

---

## Notes

1. See Richard Neitzel Holzapfel, "Thou Shalt Remember: The Eleventh Commandment," CES Symposium on the Old Testament, 1991 (Salt Lake City: Church Educational System, 1991), 6–7.

2. S. Kent Brown's works on the Exodus pattern, especially in relationship to the Book of Mormon, are an important scholarly effort; see for example, S. Kent Brown, "Trust in the Lord: Exodus and Faith," in *The Old Testament and the Latter-day Saints* [Sperry Symposium 1986] (Salt Lake City: Randall

Book Company, 1986), pp. 85–94; "The Exodus Pattern in the Book of Mormon," *BYU Studies,* Summer 1990, pp. 111–26.

3. See "Exodus, Book of" Bible Dictionary, p. 668.

4. See, for example, 1 Nephi 17:23–32.

5. Since my presentation at the 1987 CES annual scripture symposium, others have published articles dealing with this theme and in some cases have expanded upon it; see for example Thomas R. Valletta's 1994 essay, "The Exodus: Prophetic Type and the Plan of Redemption," in *Thy People Shall Be My People And Thy God My God: The 22d Annual Sidney B. Sperry Symposium* (Salt Lake City: Deseret Book Company, 1994), pp. 178–90.

6. BYU ancient scripture professor Victor L. Ludlow observed: "To better appreciate these five books, review them from the context of the Israelites during the time of Moses and note how these detailed, particular instructions were necessary to separate them from their Egyptian paganism and to prepare them for their settlement in the promised land (note that the Jaredites, Nephites, and Mormon pioneers also went through long periods of travel, testing, and teaching before they reached their own lands of promise). Then try to evaluate the principles or higher laws behind all the laws, commandments, and stories of this period of Israelite history. Finally, try to apply these principles and higher laws to life today and compare them to the laws of the gospel. Such a threefold approach to this material will take it from the realm of dry, historical past and place it within the struggles and challenges of contemporary life." (*Unlocking the Old Testament* [Salt Lake City: Deseret Book Company, 1981], p. 22.)

CHAPTER ONE

# The Exodus Story

*T*he book of Exodus begins: "Now these are the names of the children of Israel, which came into Egypt; every man and his household came with Jacob. Reuben, Simeon, Levi, and Judah, Issachar, Zebulun, and Benjamin, Dan, and Naphtali, Gad, and Asher." (Exodus 1:1–4.) The record adds: "And all the souls that came out of the loins of Jacob were seventy souls: for Joseph was in Egypt already" (Exodus 1:5). As a continuation of Genesis, as these verses demonstrate, Exodus is the unfolding of God's work to fulfill the covenant he established with Abram (Abraham).

Genesis tells us that Abram (the name means "exalted father") migrated to Haran and eventually to Canaan. His journey to Canaan, his call, and the reception of the covenant from the Lord are recorded in Genesis 12:1–5. Eventually, Abram received further blessings and promises from the Lord (see Genesis 15:1; 17:8). As a token of the covenant, the Lord instituted circumcision and changed Abram's name to Abraham (which means "father of a multitude"). Later, the Lord asked Abraham to offer his son Isaac as a sacrifice. When Abraham obeyed, the Lord renewed the earlier promises and blessings (see Genesis 22). As a result, Abraham is the father of the faithful, who are personified in the House of Israel, God's covenant people.

One particular aspect of the covenant blessings Abraham received was an eternal inheritance of certain lands (see Genesis 17; 22:15–18; Galatians 3; Abraham 2). It was from this promised land that his descendants left to go into the land of Egypt at the behest of Abraham's great-grandson, Joseph.

The book of Exodus indicates that "the children of Israel were fruitful, and increased abundantly, and multiplied, and waxed exceeding mighty; and the land was filled with them" (Exodus 1:7). Again, Exodus reveals the continuing fulfillment of the Lord's promises made to his servants and God's promised blessings to Adam and Eve (see Genesis 1:28), Noah (see Genesis 8:17), Abraham (see Genesis 17:2), Isaac (see Genesis 26:4), and Jacob (see Genesis 28:14; 35:11; 48:4) of fruitfulness and increase. Yet, within time:

> There arose up a new king over Egypt, which knew not Joseph. And he said unto his people, Behold, the people of the children of Israel are more and mightier than we: Come on, let us deal wisely with them; lest they multiply, and it come to pass, that, when there falleth out any war, they join also unto our enemies, and fight against us, and so get them up out of the land. Therefore they did set over them taskmasters to afflict them with their burdens. And they built for Pharaoh treasure cities, Pithom and Raamses. But the more they afflicted them, the more they multiplied and grew. And they were grieved because of the children of Israel. (Exodus 1:8–12.)

Apparently it was several hundred years from the death of Joseph to the time when "there arose up a new king over Egypt." The new king, probably Ahmose, I, the founder of the eighteenth dynasty who expelled the predominantly Semitic rulers of Egypt (then known as Hyksos), is the archetypal anti-hero who tries to thwart God's promises.[1] The story continues: "The Egyptians made the children of Israel to serve with rigour: and they made their lives bitter with hard bondage, in morter, and in brick, and in all manner of service in the field: all their service, wherein they made them serve, was with rigour" (Exodus 1:13–14). This aspect of the story is commemorated in the Passover meal with the "bitter herbs" served (see Exodus 12:8).

Making their lives "bitter with hard bondage" was not enough, however. Pharaoh demanded that the midwives kill all the newborn sons of the Israelites: "And he said, When ye do the office of a midwife to the Hebrew women, and see them upon the stools [two rocks a woman sat upon during childbirth]; if it be a son, then ye shall kill him: but if it be a daughter, then she shall live" (Exodus 1:16).

Of course, the midwives did not listen to Pharaoh because they "feared God" (Exodus 1:17). Again, his efforts to destroy the promises of God failed. Pharaoh then commanded "all his people, saying, Every son that is born ye shall cast into the river, and every daughter ye shall save alive" (Exodus 1:22).

At this time, among the Israelites was a "man of the house of Levi" who married a "daughter of Levi" (Exodus 2:1). The couple had a male child, which they hid for three months, and "when she could not longer hide him, she took for him an ark of bulrushes, and daubed it with slime and with pitch, and put the child therein; and she laid it in the flags by the river's brink. And his sister stood afar off, to wit what would be done to him." (Exodus 2:3–4.)

The narrative continues as "the daughter of Pharaoh came down to wash herself at the river; . . . and when she saw the ark among the flags, she sent her maid to fetch it. And when she had opened it, she saw the child: and, behold, the babe wept. And she had compassion on him." (Exodus 2:5–6.) The daughter of Pharaoh, possibly the eighteenth-dynasty princess who later became Queen Hatshepsut, raised the young child, whom she called Moses, to manhood. Again, Pharaoh is thwarted in his plan to destroy Moses. Incidentally, all the efforts by Pharaoh are frustrated by women: the midwives, the Israelite women, Moses' mother and sister, and finally his own daughter.

The story of Moses' remarkable deliverance foreshadows Israel's eventual deliverance; it is a parallel within a parallel. Additionally, the story reveals Pharaoh's inability to destroy those who God has called (Moses and the Israelites), and the word play on Moses' name reminds the reader of the deliverance of Israel by the Lord at the Red Sea" (see Exodus 13:17–14:31).

Additionally, the parallel between this event and the killing of "all the children that were in Bethlehem, and in all the coasts thereof" (see Matthew 2:16–18) at the time of Jesus' birth is striking. For Matthew, Jesus was the new Moses; his life and labors were foreshadowed in the life of Moses and played out during the ministry of the mortal Messiah. We will discuss this in more detail in the following chapter.

Eventually, Moses fled Egypt from Pharaoh (probably Thutmose III) to dwell in the land of Madian [Midian] when he was about forty years old.[2] The scriptures indicate that Moses lived in the land of Madian forty years (see Acts 7:29–30). Meanwhile back in Egypt, the "king of Egypt died: and the children of Israel sighed by reason of the bondage, and they cried, and their cry came up unto God by reason of the bondage. And God heard their groaning, and God remembered his covenant with Abraham, with Isaac, and with Jacob. And God looked upon the children of Israel, and God had respect unto them." (Exodus 2:23–25.)

The story returns to Moses as God calls him to full-time service in his cause to bring about Israel's deliverance:

> Now Moses kept the flock of Jethro his father in law, the priest of Midian: and he led the flock to the backside of the desert, and came to the mountain of God, even to Horeb [possibly an alternative name for Mount Sinai].
>
> And the angel of the Lord appeared unto him in a flame of fire out of the midst of a bush: and he looked, and, behold, the bush burned with fire, and the bush was not consumed.
>
> And Moses said, I will now turn aside, and see this great sight, why the bush is not burnt.
>
> And when the Lord saw that he turned aside to see, God called unto him out of the midst of the bush, and said, Moses, Moses. And he said, Here am I.

And he said, Draw not nigh hither: put off thy shoes from off thy feet, for the place whereon thou standest is holy ground. (Exodus 3:1–5.)

Like father Jacob (Israel) and like the future king of Israel (David), Moses watched over a flock of sheep, a preparation for his call to be the shepherd of Israel. The Lord told him: "I am the God of thy father, the God of Abraham, the God of Isaac, and the God of Jacob. And Moses hid his face; for he was afraid to look upon God. And the Lord said, I have surely seen the affliction of my people which are in Egypt, and have heard their cry by reason of their taskmasters; for I know their sorrows; and I am come down to deliver them out of the hand of the Egyptians, and to bring them up out of that land unto a good land and a large, unto a land flowing with milk and honey." (Exodus 3:6–8.)

Moses' call continues: "Now therefore, behold, the cry of the children of Israel is come unto me: and I have also seen the oppression wherewith the Egyptians oppress them. Come now therefore, and I will send thee unto Pharaoh, that thou mayest bring forth my people the children of Israel out of Egypt." (Exodus 3:9–10.) After a brief protest by Moses, the Lord said: "Certainly I will be with thee; and this shall be a token unto thee, that I have sent thee: When thou hast brought forth the people out of Egypt, ye shall serve God upon this mountain" (Exodus 3:12). The Lord further announced: "And I will stretch out my hand, and smite Egypt with all my wonders which I will do in the midst thereof: and after that he will let you go" (Exodus 3:20).

Eventually, "Moses took his wife and his sons, . . . and he returned to the land of Egypt: and Moses took the rod of God in his hand" (Exodus 4:20). In Egypt, Moses and Aaron "went and gathered together all the elders of the children of Israel: and Aaron spake all the words which the Lord had spoken unto Moses, and did the signs in the sight of the people. And the people believed: and when they heard that the Lord had visited the children of Israel, and that he had looked upon their affliction, then they bowed their heads and worshipped." (Exodus 4:29–31.)

A new section begins when Moses and Aaron approach Pharaoh and demand in the name of the Lord that he let the people go. Pharaoh's response to the demand is general and specific. First he asks, "Who is the Lord, that I should obey his voice to let Israel go?" (Exodus 5:2.) More specifically, he then says: "I know not the Lord, neither will I let Israel go" (Exodus 5:2).

After the encounter between Pharaoh and the two brothers, the ruler of Egypt tries to prevent the Israelites from listening to Moses and Aaron by a plan which he hopes will turn the Israelites against the brothers: "And Pharaoh commanded the same day the taskmasters of the people, and their officers, saying, Ye shall no more give the people straw to make brick, as heretofore: let them go and gather straw for themselves. And the tale of the bricks, which they did make heretofore, ye shall lay upon them; ye shall not diminish ought thereof: for they be idle; therefore they cry, saying, Let us go and sacrifice to our God. Let there more work be laid upon the men, that they may labour therein; and let them not regard vain words." (Exodus 5:6–9.)

Immediately following the issuance of the decree, "the taskmasters of the people went out, and their officers, and they spake to the people, saying, Thus saith Pharaoh, I will not give you straw. Go ye, get you straw where ye can find it: yet not ought of your work shall be diminished." (Exodus 5:10–11.) The helpless Israelite slaves were then compelled to bear additional burdens: "So the people were scattered abroad throughout all the land of Egypt to gather stubble instead of straw. And the taskmasters hasted them, saying, Fulfil your works, your daily tasks, as when there was straw. And the officers of the children of Israel, which Pharaoh's taskmasters had set over them, were beaten, and demanded, Wherefore have ye not fulfilled your task in making brick both yesterday and to day, as heretofore?" (Exodus 5:12–14.)

As the tension grew, Moses and Aaron met the Israelite officers, whose resentment toward the brothers, as Pharaoh hoped, had reached a fevered pitch, so much so that the officers blamed Moses and Aaron for making life harder and for putting "a sword in [the Egyptians'] hand to slay us" (Exodus 5:21). The tension reached its climax as Moses turned to the Lord and asked why matters had turned for the worse. The Lord responds: "Now shalt thou see what I will do to Pharaoh: for with a strong hand shall he let them go, and with a strong hand shall he drive them out of his land. . . . And I have also established my covenant with them, to give them the land of Canaan, the land of their pilgrimage, wherein they were strangers. And I have also heard the groaning of the children of Israel, whom the Egyptians keep in bondage; and I have remembered my covenant." (Exodus 6:1, 4–5.)

The next scripture is important as a threefold reminder of God's purpose: "Wherefore say unto the children of Israel, I am the Lord, and I will bring you out from under the burdens of the Egyptians, and I will rid you out of their bondage, and I will redeem you with a stretched out arm, and with great judgments: and I will take you to me for a people, and I will be to you a God: and ye shall know that I am the Lord your God, which bringeth you out from under the burdens of the Egyptians. And I will bring you in unto the land, concerning the which I did swear to give it to Abraham, to Isaac, and to Jacob; and I will give it you for an heritage: I am the Lord." (Exodus 6:6–8.)

The record indicates that Moses was eighty years old and Aaron was eighty-three years old when these events took place (see Exodus 7:7).

The next part of the story is one of the major focal points of the book of Exodus. Here God announces judgment against Egypt for enslaving his covenant people: "And the Lord spake unto Moses and unto Aaron, saying, When Pharaoh shall speak unto you, saying, Shew a miracle for you: then thou shalt say unto Aaron, Take thy rod, and cast it before Pharaoh, and it shall become a serpent. And Moses and Aaron went in unto Pharaoh, and they did so as the Lord had commanded: and

Aaron cast down his rod before Pharaoh, and before his servants, and it became a serpent. Then Pharaoh also called the wise men and the sorcerers: now the magicians of Egypt, they also did in like manner with their enchantments. For they cast down every man his rod, and they became serpents: but Aaron's rod swallowed up their rods." (Exodus 7:8–12.)

In the end, as the Lord had prophesied, "Pharaoh hardened his heart, that he hearkened not unto them" (JST, Exodus 7:13). The Lord proceeds to inform Moses that since Pharaoh's heart is stubborn (the sense of the word *harden* here) and will not "let the people go" (Exodus 7:14), there was no other way but to inflict on the Egyptians the plagues that would punish them for their acts against Israel and impel them step by step to the final prophesied outcome of freeing the slaves so they could worship the Lord at his mountain.

The first nine plagues, also called signs and wonders, can be divided into three groups of three judgments each (see Exodus 7:14–18:19; 8:20–9:12; 9:13–10:29), with the first plague in each group (the first, the fourth, and the seventh) introduced by a warning delivered to Pharaoh by Moses in the morning as Pharaoh went out to the Nile (see Exodus 7:15; 8:20; 9:13). These plagues climax with the tenth and final plague, the death of the eldest sons.

The step-by-step movement toward the defeat of Egypt's gods (see Exodus 12:12 and Numbers 33:4) and of Pharaoh himself by God's outstretched arm and mighty hand begins in Exodus 7:

> Get thee unto Pharaoh in the morning; lo, he goeth out unto the water; and thou shalt stand by the river's brink against he come; and the rod which was turned to a serpent shalt thou take in thine hand.
>
> And thou shalt say unto him, The Lord God of the Hebrews hath sent me unto thee, saying, Let my people go, that they may serve me in the wilderness: and, behold, hitherto thou wouldest not hear.
>
> Thus saith the Lord, In this thou shalt know that I am the Lord: behold, I will smite with the rod that is in mine hand upon the waters which are in the river, and they shall be turned to blood.

And the fish that is in the river shall die, and the river shall stink; and the Egyptians shall lothe to drink of the water of the river.

And the Lord spake unto Moses, Say unto Aaron, Take thy rod, and stretch out thine hand upon the waters of Egypt, upon their streams, upon their rivers, and upon their ponds, and upon all their pools of water, that they may become blood; and that there may be blood throughout all the land of Egypt, both in the vessels of wood, and in vessels of stone.

And Moses and Aaron did so, as the Lord commanded; and he lifted up the rod, and smote the waters that were in the river, in the sight of Pharaoh, and in the sight of his servants; and all the waters that were in the river were turned to blood.

And the fish that was in the river died; and the river stank, and the Egyptians could not drink of the water of the river; and there was blood throughout all the land of Egypt. (Exodus 7:15–21.)

When magicians of Egypt attempted to invoke their enchantments they failed, demonstrating the Lord's power over the forces of darkness. When seven days were fulfilled, the Lord spoke to Moses again:

Go unto Pharaoh, and say unto him, Thus saith the Lord, Let my people go, that they may serve me.

And if thou refuse to let them go, behold, I will smite all thy borders with frogs:

And the river shall bring forth frogs abundantly, which shall go up and come into thine house, and into thy bedchamber, and upon thy bed, and into the house of thy servants, and upon thy people, and into thine ovens, and into thy kneadingtroughs:

And the frogs shall come up both on thee, and upon thy people, and upon all thy servants.

And the Lord spake unto Moses, Say unto Aaron, Stretch forth thine hand with thy rod over the streams, over the rivers, and over the ponds, and cause frogs to come up upon the land of Egypt.

And Aaron stretched out his hand over the waters of Egypt; and the frogs came up, and covered the land of Egypt. (Exodus 8:1–6.)

Again, the magicians failed in their attempt to stop the plague. This time, however, "Pharaoh called for Moses and Aaron, and said, Intreat the Lord, that he may take away the frogs from me, and from my people; and I will let the people go, that they may do sacrifice unto the Lord" (Exodus 8:8). Yet following the respite, Pharaoh again hardened his heart "and hearkened not unto them; as the Lord had said" (Exodus 8:15).

The Lord sent another plague, a scourge of lice: "And the Lord said unto Moses, Say unto Aaron, Stretch out thy rod, and smite the dust of the land, that it may become lice throughout all the land of Egypt. And they did so; for Aaron stretched out his hand with his rod, and smote the dust of the earth, and it became lice in man, and in beast; all the dust of the land became lice throughout all the land of Egypt." (Exodus 8:16–17.)

Despite the pleas of the magicians, "Pharaoh's heart was hardened, and he hearkened not unto them; as the Lord had said" (Exodus 8:19). The Lord commanded Moses again:

> Rise up early in the morning, and stand before Pharaoh; lo, he cometh forth to the water; and say unto him, Thus saith the Lord, Let my people go, that they may serve me.
>
> Else, if thou wilt not let my people go, behold, I will send swarms of flies upon thee, and upon thy servants, and upon thy people, and into thy houses: and the houses of the Egyptians shall be full of swarms of flies, and also the ground whereon they are.
>
> And I will sever in that day the land of Goshen, in which my people dwell, that no swarms of flies shall be there; to the end thou mayest know that I am the Lord in the midst of the earth.
>
> And I will put a division between my people and thy people: to morrow shall this sign be.
>
> And the Lord did so; and there came a grievous swarm of flies into the house of Pharaoh, and into his servants' houses, and into all the land of Egypt: the land was corrupted by reason of the swarm of flies. (Exodus 8:20–24.)

Pharaoh called "for Moses and for Aaron, and said, Go ye, sacrifice to your God in the land," but Moses refused, saying, "It is not meet so to do; for we shall sacrifice the abomination of the Egyptians to the Lord our God: lo, shall we sacrifice the abomination of the Egyptians before their eyes, and will they not stone us? We will go three days' journey into the wilderness, and sacrifice to the Lord our God, as he shall command us." (Exodus 8:25–27.)

Upon acceptance of the proposal, Moses promised to "intreat the Lord that the swarms of flies may depart from Pharaoh, from his servants, and from his people, to morrow" (Exodus 8:29), but warned Pharaoh not to renege. The scriptures woefully record, "Pharaoh hardened his heart at this time also, neither would he let the people go" (Exodus 8:32).

Then the Lord spoke to Moses again: "Go in unto Pharaoh, and tell him, Thus saith the Lord God of the Hebrews, Let my people go, that they may serve me. For if thou refuse to let them go, and wilt hold them still, Behold, the hand of the Lord is upon thy cattle which is in the field, upon the horses, upon the asses, upon the camels, upon the oxen, and upon the sheep: there shall be a very grievous murrain. And the Lord shall sever between the cattle of Israel and the cattle of Egypt: and there shall nothing die of all that is the children's of Israel." (Exodus 9:1–4.)

Another plague is announced as Moses is commanded to "sprinkle [ashes] toward the heaven in the sight of Pharaoh. And it shall become small dust in all the land of Egypt, and shall be a boil breaking forth with blains upon man, and upon beast, throughout all the land of Egypt. And they took ashes of the furnace, and stood before Pharaoh; and Moses sprinkled it up toward heaven; and it became a boil breaking forth with blains upon man, and upon beast." (Exodus 9:8–10.)

The symbolic reason for taking the ashes from the furnace may be an effort to remind the Egyptians that the Israelites fired their brick in furnaces. Additionally, the word *furnace* is used as a simile for the destruction of Sodom and Gomorrah (see Genesis 19:28).

In the end, the "magicians could not stand before Moses because of the boils; for the boil was upon the magicians, and upon all the Egyptians" (Exodus 9:11). Despite this devastating plague of probable skin anthrax, Pharaoh "hearkened not unto" Moses and Aaron, "as the Lord had spoken" (Exodus 9:12).

Again, the Lord spoke to Moses, commanding him to appear before Pharaoh and to speak in the name of Israel's God:

> Thus saith the Lord God of the Hebrews, Let my people go, that they may serve me.
>
> For I will at this time send all my plagues upon thine heart, and upon thy servants, and upon thy people; that thou mayest know that there is none like me in all the earth.
>
> For now I will stretch out my hand, that I may smite thee and thy people with pestilence; and thou shalt be cut off from the earth.
>
> And in very deed for this cause have I raised thee up, for to shew in thee my power; and that my name may be declared throughout all the earth.
>
> As yet exaltest thou thyself against my people, that thou wilt not let them go?
>
> Behold, to morrow about this time I will cause it to rain a very grievous hail, such as hath not been in Egypt since the foundation thereof even until now.
>
> Send therefore now, and gather thy cattle, and all that thou hast in the field; for upon every man and beast which shall be found in the field, and shall not be brought home, the hail shall come down upon them, and they shall die. (Exodus 9:13–19.)

Again, Pharaoh called "for Moses and Aaron, and said unto them, I have sinned this time: the Lord is righteous, and I and my people are wicked" (Exodus 9:27). This is the first time that Pharaoh announces his culpability in subjecting God's covenant people into bitter bondage. He then asks Moses to entreat the Lord to stop the plague, and he promises that he will let the people go. Moses responds: "As soon as I am gone out of the city, I will spread abroad my hands unto the Lord; and the thunder shall cease, neither shall there be any more hail; that thou mayest know how that the earth is the Lord's" (Exodus 9:29). And as the Lord had already prophesied, when the effects of the plague stopped, "Pharaoh . . . hardened his heart, . . . neither would he let the children of Israel go" (Exodus 9:34–35).

Chapter ten begins as the Lord commands Moses to go before Pharaoh another time. The Lord informs Moses that the stories about Egyptian bondage and ultimate deliverance by the Lord are to be told and retold:

> And that thou mayest tell in the ears of thy son, and of thy son's son, what things I have wrought in Egypt, and my signs which I have done among them; that ye may know how that I am the Lord.
>
> And Moses and Aaron came in unto Pharaoh, and said unto him, Thus saith the Lord God of the Hebrews, How long wilt thou refuse to humble thyself before me? let my people go, that they may serve me.
>
> Else, if thou refuse to let my people go, behold, to morrow will I bring the locusts into thy coast:
>
> And they shall cover the face of the earth, that one cannot be able to see the earth: and they shall eat the residue of that which is escaped, which remaineth unto you from the hail, and shall eat every tree which groweth for you out of the field:
>
> And they shall fill thy houses, and the houses of all thy servants, and the houses of all the Egyptians; which neither thy fathers, nor thy fathers' fathers have seen, since the day that they were upon the earth unto this day. And he turned himself, and went out from Pharaoh.
>
> And Pharaoh's servants said unto him, How long shall this man be a snare unto us? let the men go, that they may serve the Lord their God: knowest thou not yet that Egypt is destroyed? (Exodus 10:2–7.)

Ironically, Pharaoh's servants echo the same words of the prophet himself, "How long?" Additionally, they foresee the inevitable result of not hearkening unto the Lord's commandments: "Egypt is destroyed." Pharaoh brought Moses and Aaron back and ordered them to leave and "go, serve the Lord your God" (Exodus 10:8) with one stipulation: they were to allow only the men to leave. Apparently this stipulation was rejected, and Moses and Aaron were "driven out from Pharaoh's presence" (Exodus 10:11). At this, the Lord commanded Moses: "Stretch out thine hand over the land of Egypt for the locusts, that they may come up upon the land of Egypt, and eat every herb of the land, even all that the hail hath left" (Exodus 10:12).

The drama continues as Pharaoh "called for Moses and Aaron in haste" (Exodus 10:16). He pleads with them to "intreat the Lord your God, that he may take away from me this death only" (Exodus 10:17). In another reversal that is utterly unfathomable, Pharaoh again turns against the Lord and, as the scripture states, "would not let the children of Israel go" (Exodus 10:20).

The next plague, like the third and sixth ones, are not revealed to Pharaoh in advance: "And Moses stretched forth his hand toward heaven; and there was a thick darkness in all the land of Egypt three days: They saw not one another, neither rose any from his place for three days: but all the children of Israel had light in their dwellings" (Exodus 10:22–23).

In what can be seen as an ironic statement made during the time of total darkness, Pharaoh commands Moses: "Get thee from me, take heed to thyself, see my face no more; for in that day thou seest my face thou shalt die" (Exodus 10:28).

With this, the Lord announces to Moses one last tragic plague: "Yet will I bring one plague more upon Pharaoh, and upon Egypt" (Exodus 11:1). This ultimate disaster which falls upon Egypt forces Pharaoh to, in the Lord's words, "let you go hence: when he shall let you go, he shall surely thrust you out hence altogether" (Exodus 11:1). To the Israelites, Moses announces the last judgment upon Pharaoh and all the Egyptians: "Thus saith the Lord, About midnight will I go out into the midst of Egypt: and all the firstborn in the land of Egypt shall die, from the firstborn of Pharaoh that sitteth upon his throne, even unto the firstborn of the maidservant that is behind the mill; and all the firstborn of beasts. And there shall be a great cry throughout all the land of Egypt, such as there was none like it, nor shall be like it any more." (Exodus 11:4–6.)

Yet, "against any of the children of Israel shall not a dog move his tongue, against man or beast: that ye may know how that the Lord doth put a difference between the Egyptians and Israel" (Exodus 11:7). And then, prophesies Moses, the Egyptians will bow before Moses and say: "Get thee out, and all the people that follow thee: and after that I will go out" (Exodus 11:8).

This was a new beginning, a day of liberation and freedom. The Lord declares, "This month shall be unto you the beginning of months: it shall be the first month of the year to you" (Exodus 12:2). Israel's religious calendar is established to remind the children of Jacob that their lives as the people of the Lord are rooted in God's redemptive act in the exodus.

In the celebration of this act, the Israelites were commanded to gather together, and each family "shall take to them every man a lamb, according to the house of their fathers, a lamb for an house" (Exodus 12:3). Specifically, the lamb "shall be without blemish, a male of the first year: ye shall take it out from the sheep, or from the goats" (Exodus 12:5).

The commandment concerning the ceremony continues: "And the whole assembly of the congregation of Israel shall kill it in the evening. And they shall take of the blood, and strike it on the two side posts and on the upper door post of the houses, wherein they shall eat it. And they shall eat the flesh in that night, roast with fire, and unleavened bread; and with bitter herbs they shall eat it. Eat not of it raw, nor sodden at all with water, but roast with fire; his head with his legs, and with the purtenance thereof. And ye shall let nothing of it remain until the morning; and that which remaineth of it until the morning ye shall burn with fire. And thus shall ye eat it; with your loins girded, your shoes on your feet, and your staff in your hand; and ye shall eat it in haste: it is the Lord's passover." (Exodus 12:6–11.)

The elements of blood, bitter herbs, roasting, and unleavened bread remind Israel of special aspects of the story. The blood symbolizes the sacrifice offered as a substitution, one life laid down for another (see Leviticus 17:11). Therefore, through the mediation of a sacrifice the children of Israel escape the judgment which is about to fall upon the Egyptians (see Hebrews 9:22; 1 John 1:7). The bitter herbs, as already noted, remind Israel of the bitter years of bondage. The roasting of the lamb, the typical method of cooking a lamb by shepherds, recalls the earlier life of Abraham, the wandering shepherd looking for the promised land. Finally, unleavened bread recalls the haste with which the people would leave Egypt.

The Lord explains why it is called the Lord's passover: "For I will pass through the land of Egypt this night, and will smite all the firstborn in the land of Egypt, both man and beast; and against all the gods of Egypt I will execute judgment: I am the Lord. And the blood shall be to you for a token upon the houses where ye are: and when I see the blood, I will pass over you, and the plague shall not be upon you to destroy you, when I smite the land of Egypt." (Exodus 12:12–13; see also 12:23, 27.)

Just as the plagues were signs to Pharaoh and the Egyptians of the Lord's judgment (see Exodus 8:23), so the blood on the doorpost was a sign or token of God's mercy.

The Lord commanded the Israelites to celebrate their deliverance annually: "And this day shall be unto you for a memorial; and ye shall keep it a feast to the Lord throughout your generations; ye shall keep it a feast by an ordinance for ever" (Exodus 12:14).

In words that emphasize the fulfillment of prophecy, Moses continues his record: "And it came to pass, that at midnight the Lord smote all the firstborn in the land of Egypt, from the firstborn of Pharaoh that sat on his throne unto the firstborn of the captive that was in the dungeon; and all the firstborn of cattle" (Exodus 12:29).

Finally, Pharaoh, who had commanded Moses never to appear before him again on the penalty of death, called "for Moses and Aaron by night, and said, Rise up, and get you forth from among my people, both ye and the children of Israel; and go, serve the Lord, as ye have said. Also take your flocks and your herds, as ye have said, and be gone; and bless me also. And the Egyptians were urgent upon the people, that they might send them out of the land in haste; for they said, We be all dead men." (Exodus 12:31–33.)

The narrative notes the following at this point: "And it came to pass at the end of the four hundred and thirty years, even the selfsame day it came to pass, that all the hosts of the Lord went out from the land of Egypt" (Exodus 12:41). Putting it in perspective, the narrative adds: "And it came to pass the selfsame day, that the Lord did bring the children of Israel out of the land of Egypt by their armies" (Exodus 12:51).

Not only were Egypt's gods defeated by the Lord, but Pharaoh himself. The expressions "with an outstretched arm" and a "mighty hand" take on a special meaning when it is realized that similar expressions are found in Egyptian literature that symbolize the conquering and controlling power of Pharaoh. In this sense, the story revolves around the struggle between the Lord and Pharaoh, known in Egypt as the "Son of Re," "Good God," and other divine titles. Of course, the death of the firstborn, including Pharaoh's own son, is one of the culminating defeats. The final assault on Pharaoh's power and authority came at the Red Sea. The Lord says: "He shall follow after them; and I will be honoured upon Pharaoh, and upon all his host; that the Egyptians may know that I am the Lord" (Exodus 14:4).

Note specifically how Jethro places the events in this context, "Blessed be the Lord, who hath delivered you out of the hand of the Egyptians, and out of the hand of Pharaoh, who hath delivered the people from under the hand of the Egyptians" (Exodus 18:10). In the end, the people "know that the Lord is greater than all gods: for in the thing wherein they dealt proudly he was above them" (Exodus 18:11).

On the fateful day, Moses told the people: "Remember this day, in which ye came out from Egypt, out of the house of bondage; for by strength of hand the Lord brought you out from this place: there shall no leavened bread be eaten" (Exodus 13:3).

Finally, "God led the people about, through the way of the wilderness of the Red sea: and the children of Israel went up harnessed out of the land of Egypt" (Exodus 13:18). The scripture indicates that "the Lord went before them by day in a pillar of a cloud, to lead them the way; and by night in a pillar of fire, to give them light; to go by day and night: he took not away the pillar of the cloud by day, nor the pillar of fire by night, from before the people" (Exodus 13:21–22).

As already noted, when Pharaoh pursued the Israelites, the Lord confronted the Egyptians one last time: "And Moses stretched out his hand over the sea; and the Lord caused the sea to go back by a strong east wind all that night, and made the sea dry land, and the waters were divided. And the children of Israel went into the midst of the sea upon the dry ground: and the waters were a wall unto them on their right hand, and on their left." (Exodus 14:21–22.) Again, Moses emphasizes: "Thus the Lord saved Israel that day out of the hand of the Egyptians; and Israel saw the Egyptians dead upon the sea shore" (Exodus 14:30). Having defeated the Egyptians, the Israelites "believed the Lord, and his servant Moses" (Exodus 14:31).

The importance of this chapter is more than the preservation of a dramatic intervention; it is the introduction of two important themes which appear throughout the wilderness narrative. The first theme is that the Israelites regret that they left Egypt (see Exodus 14:11–12). The second is the emphasis on the salvation that God alone can give and that his people must accept in faith (see Exodus 14:13–14).

One of the most beautiful songs of redemption in scripture is found at this point. Commonly called the "Song of the Sea" by scholars, this hymn of praise is also known as "A Paean of Victory," or simply as "Song of Moses." The poetic hymn of Exodus 15 is sung by Moses and the Israelites as though one person, the whole community praises God for the deliverance from bondage:

> Then sang Moses and the children of Israel this song unto the Lord, and spake, saying, I will sing unto the Lord, for he hath triumphed gloriously: the horse and his rider hath he thrown into the sea.

The Lord is my strength and song, and he is become my salvation: he is my God, and I will prepare him an habitation; my father's God, and I will exalt him.

The Lord is a man of war: the Lord is his name.

Pharaoh's chariots and his host hath he cast into the sea: his chosen captains also are drowned in the Red sea.

The depths have covered them: they sank into the bottom as a stone.

Thy right hand, O Lord, is become glorious in power: thy right hand, O Lord, hath dashed in pieces the enemy.

And in the greatness of thine excellency thou hast overthrown them that rose up against thee: thou sentest forth thy wrath, which consumed them as stubble.

And with the blast of thy nostrils the waters were gathered together, the floods stood upright as an heap, and the depths were congealed in the heart of the sea.

The enemy said, I will pursue, I will overtake, I will divide the spoil; my lust shall be satisfied upon them; I will draw my sword, my hand shall destroy them.

Thou didst blow with thy wind, the sea covered them: they sank as lead in the mighty waters.

Who is like unto thee, O Lord, among the gods? who is like thee, glorious in holiness, fearful in praises, doing wonders?

Thou stretchedst out thy right hand, the earth swallowed them.

Thou in thy mercy hast led forth the people which thou hast redeemed: thou hast guided them in thy strength unto thy holy habitation.

The people shall hear, and be afraid: sorrow shall take hold on the inhabitants of Palestina.

Then the dukes of Edom shall be amazed; the mighty men of Moab, trembling shall take hold upon them; all the inhabitants of Canaan shall melt away.

Fear and dread shall fall upon them; by the greatness of thine arm they shall be as still as a stone; till thy people pass over, O Lord, till the people pass over, which thou hast purchased.

Thou shalt bring them in, and plant them in the mountain of thine inheritance, in the place, O Lord, which thou hast made for thee to dwell in, in the Sanctuary, O Lord, which thy hands have established.

The Lord shall reign for ever and ever.

For the horse of Pharaoh went in with his chariots and with his horsemen into the sea, and the Lord brought again the waters of the sea upon them; but the children of Israel went on dry land in the midst of the sea. (Exodus 15:1–19.)

Ironically, the Israelites, who had just been saved from bitter bondage through the Lord's goodness and mercy, almost immediately began to murmur when they entered Sinai, the large, wedge-shaped block of land that forms a major land bridge between Africa and Asia. Sinai's climate is hostile, and in the traditional location for the wilderness of Sinai, the south-central part of the peninsula, the Israelites were brought into a region which necessitated their reliance upon the Lord in order to survive. Apparently, this is one of the reasons why the Lord brought them into the wilderness.

First, they had want of bread and second they had want of water (see Exodus 16–17). In both cases, the Lord provided for their needs, thus demonstrating the value of placing their faith and hopes on his promises. "Then said the Lord unto Moses, Behold, I will rain bread from heaven for you; and the people shall go out and gather a certain rate every day, that I may prove them, whether they will walk in my law, or no. . . . And the Lord said unto Moses, Go on before the people, and take with thee of the elders of Israel; and thy rod, wherewith thou smotest the river, take in thine hand, and go. Behold, I will stand before thee there upon the rock in Horeb; and thou shalt smite the rock, and there shall come water out of it, that the people may drink." (Exodus 16:4; 17:5–6.)

A new section begins in Exodus 19: "In the third month, when the children of Israel were gone forth out of the land of Egypt, the same day came they into the wilderness of Sinai" (Exodus 19:1). The remaining part of the story recorded in Exodus, all of Leviticus, and Numbers 1:1–10:10 occurs here, in the southeast region of the peninsula.

With striking cadence we learn: "For they were departed from Rephidim, and were come to the desert of Sinai, and had pitched in the wilderness; and there Israel camped before the mount" (Exodus 19:2). This mount is known to biblical writers by several names— "mountain of God," "Mount Horeb"—but its exact location is still unknown, though a traditional site has been identified.[4] Moses ascends the mountain, as he had done before, and meets the Lord, who speaks: "Thus shalt thou say to the house of Jacob, and tell the children of Israel; ye have seen what I did unto the Egyptians, and how I bare you on eagles' wings, and brought you unto myself. Now therefore, if ye will obey my voice indeed, and keep my covenant, then ye shall be a peculiar treasure unto me above all people: for all the earth is mine: and ye shall be unto me a kingdom of priests, and an holy nation. These are the words which thou shalt speak unto the children of Israel." (Exodus 19:3–6.)

In this most important section of the book of Exodus, the Lord announces the renewal of the covenant he made with Abraham and his descendants six hundred years before. If Israel accepts the terms and conditions of the covenant, they will become "a peculiar treasure," "a kingdom of priests," and "an holy nation."[5]

Each designation has special significance. First, "a peculiar treasure" means that Israel will become a special possession and a people belonging to God. Second, "a kingdom of priests" is essentially a nation made up of kings and priests wholly consecrated to the Lord. Third, a "holy nation" because, as they will learn later, collectively and individually they must be holy because the Lord is holy: "For I am the Lord that bringeth you up out of the land of Egypt, to be your God: ye shall therefore be holy, for I am holy" (Leviticus 11:45).

The people accepted the proposition: "And all the people answered together, and said, All that the Lord hath spoken we will do" (Exodus 19:8). The Lord then commands Moses to prepare them to meet God: "And the Lord said unto Moses, Go unto the people, and sanctify them to day and to morrow, and let them wash their clothes, and be ready against the third day: for the third day the Lord will come down in the sight of all the people upon mount Sinai. And thou shalt set bounds unto the people round about, saying, Take heed to yourselves, that ye go not up into the mount, or touch the border of it." (Exodus 19:10–12.)

On the third day, the Lord who had brought them out of Egypt with outstretched arms and a mighty hand came down on the mount:

> And it came to pass on the third day in the morning, that there were thunders and lightnings, and a thick cloud upon the mount, and the voice of the trumpet exceeding loud; so that all the people that was in the camp trembled.
>
> And Moses brought forth the people out of the camp to meet with God; and they stood at the nether part of the mount.
>
> And mount Sinai was altogether on a smoke, because the Lord descended upon it in fire: and the smoke thereof ascended as the smoke of a furnace, and the whole mount quaked greatly.
>
> And when the voice of the trumpet sounded long, and waxed louder and louder, Moses spake, and God answered him by a voice.
>
> And the Lord came down upon mount Sinai, on the top of the mount: and the Lord called Moses up to the top of the mount; and Moses went up. (Exodus 19:16–20.)

In the next chapter the Lord begins to reveal his law, including the Ten Commandments, the basic law known in Hebrew as the "Ten Words" (see Exodus 20). The term Decalogue, which is often used as a synonym for the Ten Commandments, is of Greek origin and means "ten words." This important section begins boldly with the reminder: "I am the Lord thy God, which have brought thee out of the land of Egypt, out of the house of bondage" (Exodus 20:2).

The revealed law includes instructions regarding idols, altars, Hebrew servants, personal injuries, protection of property, social responsibility, laws of mercy and justice, and the three annual feasts. Of particular interest for the Exodus story parallel in the New Testament is the feasts of unleavened bread and of harvest. The Lord required: "Three times thou shalt keep a feast unto me in the year. Thou shalt keep the feast of unleavened bread: (thou shalt eat unleavened bread seven days, as I commanded thee, in the time appointed of the month Abib; for in it thou camest out from Egypt: and none shall appear before me empty:) And the feast of harvest, the firstfruits of thy labours, which thou hast sown in the field. . . . Three times in the year all thy males shall appear before the Lord." (Exodus 23:14–17.)

In Exodus 24 the covenant is confirmed:

> And he said unto Moses, Come up unto the Lord, thou, and Aaron, Nadab, and Abihu, and seventy of the elders of Israel; and worship ye afar off.
>
> And Moses alone shall come near the Lord: but they shall not come nigh; neither shall the people go up with him.
>
> And Moses came and told the people all the words of the Lord, and all the judgments: and all the people answered with one voice, and said, All the words which the Lord hath said will we do.
>
> And Moses wrote all the words of the Lord, and rose up early in the morning, and builded an altar under the hill, and twelve pillars, according to the twelve tribes of Israel.
>
> And he sent young men of the children of Israel, which offered burnt offerings, and sacrificed peace offerings of oxen unto the Lord.
>
> And Moses took half of the blood, and put it in basons; and half of the blood he sprinkled on the altar.
>
> And he took the book of the covenant, and read in the audience of the people: and they said, All that the Lord hath said will we do, and be obedient.
>
> And Moses took the blood, and sprinkled it on the people, and said, Behold the blood of the covenant, which the Lord hath made with you concerning all these words. (Exodus 24:1–8.)

Then, in one of the most remarkable passages in scripture, we learn: "Then went up Moses, and Aaron, Nadab, and Abihu, and seventy of the elders of Israel: and they saw the God of Israel: and there was under his feet as it were a paved work of a sapphire stone, and as it were the body of heaven in his clearness" (Exodus 24:9).

In preparation for their movement away from the mount, the Lord asked the Israelites for donations to build the tabernacle. Additionally, he revealed what the "tent" would look like, including the furnishings, and the duties of the priests, their clothing, and their consecration. (See Exodus 26–31.)

One of the best-known aspects of the story follows: the golden calf incident. In the very first verse of Exodus 32 we are confronted in a drastic way with the contrast between the Lord's gracious statement about the covenant—"And they shall know that I am the Lord their God, that brought them forth out of the land of Egypt, that I may dwell among them: I am the Lord their God" (Exodus 29:46)—and the people's declaration: "Make us gods, which shall go before us; for as for this Moses, the man that brought us up out of the land of Egypt, we wot not what is become of him" (Exodus 32:1).

The scripture is clear that the people have broken the covenant and therefore are disowned by the Lord, who no longer considers them his people: "And the Lord said unto Moses, Go, get thee down; for thy people, which thou broughtest out of the land of Egypt, have corrupted themselves. . . . And the Lord said unto Moses, I have seen this people, and, behold, it is a stiffnecked people." (Exodus 32:7, 9.)

Moses acts as a mediator between God and the rebellious Israelites and uses God's own words: "And Moses besought the Lord his God, and said, Lord, why doth thy wrath wax hot against *thy people,* which thou hast brought forth out of the land of Egypt with great power, and with a mighty hand?" (Exodus 32:11; emphasis added.) His pleas are heard by the Lord, and a promise is given that the Lord will be with them and that they will yet inherit the land of promise (see Exodus 33).

The book of Exodus concludes as the children of Israel fulfill the Lord's commandments to construct the tabernacle, prepare the priestly garments and the furnishings, and consecrate it as prescribed. "Then a cloud covered the tent of the congregation, and the glory of the Lord filled the tabernacle. And Moses was not able to enter into the tent of the congregation, because the cloud abode thereon, and the glory of the Lord filled the tabernacle. And when the cloud was taken up from over the tabernacle, the children of Israel went onward in all their journeys: but if the cloud were not taken up, then they journeyed not till the day that it was taken up. For the cloud of the Lord was upon the tabernacle by day, and fire was on it by night, in the sight of all the house of Israel, throughout all their journeys." (Exodus 40:34–38.)

Specifically, we learn: "And the Lord spake unto Moses and unto Aaron, saying, Every man of the children of Israel shall pitch by his own standard, with the ensign of their father's house: far off about the tabernacle of the congregation shall they pitch. . . . Then the tabernacle of the congregation shall set forward with the camp of the Levites in the midst of the camp: as they encamp, so shall they set forward, every man in his place by their standards." (Numbers 2:1–2, 17.) Thus, the tabernacle, representing God's presence, is located in the heart of the camp.

The book of Numbers informs us of the Israelites' movements during their journeys (see Numbers 10:11–33:48). The narrative finally brings us to the plains of Moab, where Moses speaks to the Israelites the words known to us as the book of Deuteronomy. Here we read of Moses' last days among the Israelites and the succession of Joshua. "And Joshua the son of Nun was full of the spirit of wisdom; for Moses had laid his hands upon him: and the children of Israel hearkened unto him, and did as the Lord commanded Moses. And there arose not a prophet since in Israel like unto Moses, whom the Lord knew face to face, in all the signs and the wonders, which the Lord sent him to do in the land of Egypt to Pharaoh, and to all his servants, and to all his land, and in all that mighty hand, and in all the great terror which Moses shewed in the sight of all Israel." (Deuteronomy 34:9–12.)

The story continues in the book of Joshua. After years of bitter bondage in Egypt and forty years in the desert, the Israelites are finally ready to enter the promised land. Joshua, pre-ordained to turn the promise to Abraham, Isaac, and Jacob into a reality, encamps on the east side of the Jordan River. The book opens with the Lord's command to move forward and pass through the river on dry land:

And the Lord said unto Joshua, This day will I begin to magnify thee in the sight of all Israel, that they may know that, as I was with Moses, so I will be with thee.

And thou shalt command the priests that bear the ark of the covenant, saying, When ye are come to the brink of the water of Jordan, ye shall stand still in Jordan.

And Joshua said unto the children of Israel, Come hither, and hear the words of the Lord your God.

And Joshua said, Hereby ye shall know that the living God is among you, and that he will without fail drive out from before you the Canaanites, and the Hittites, and the Hivites, and the Perizzites, and the Girgashites, and the Amorites, and the Jebusites.

Behold, the ark of the covenant of the Lord of all the earth passeth over before you into Jordan. . . .

And it shall come to pass, as soon as the soles of the feet of the priests that bear the ark of the Lord, the Lord of all the earth, shall rest in the waters of Jordan, that the waters of Jordan shall be cut off from the waters that come down from above; and they shall stand upon an heap. (Joshua 3:7–11, 13.)

The chapter concludes: "And the priests that bare the ark of the covenant of the Lord stood firm on dry ground in the midst of Jordan, and all the Israelites passed over on dry ground, until all the people were passed clean over Jordan" (Joshua 3:17). The Israelites placed twelve stones and were commanded to answer their children's questions about the meaning of the stones: "That the waters of Jordan were cut off before the ark of the covenant of the Lord; when it passed over Jordan, the waters of Jordan were cut off: and these stones shall be for a memorial unto the children of Israel for ever" (Joshua 4:7).

In preparation to take possession of the land, two covenantal ceremonies were resumed at Gilgal. These acts were all in accordance to the commandments given at Sinai: first, the rite of circumcision; secondly, the celebration of Passover.

The book of Joshua tells of the series of victories in central, southern, and northern Canaan that gave the Israelites control of all the hill country and the Negev. It continues with a description of the inheritances each tribe received of the Lord and ends with Joshua's final addresses to the people.

Shortly before his death, Joshua once more gathered the people together at Shechem to call Israel to a renewal of the covenant. In his final official act, Joshua speaks in the name of the Lord:

> Thus saith the Lord God of Israel, Your fathers dwelt on the other side of the flood [Euphrates River] in old time, even Terah, the father of Abraham, and the father of Nachor: and they served other gods.
>
> And I took your father Abraham from the other side of the flood, and led him throughout all the land of Canaan, and multiplied his seed, and gave him Isaac.
>
> And I gave unto Isaac Jacob and Esau: and I gave unto Esau mount Seir, to possess it; but Jacob and his children went down into Egypt.
>
> I sent Moses also and Aaron, and I plagued Egypt, according to that which I did among them: and afterward I brought you out.
>
> And I brought your fathers out of Egypt: and ye came unto the sea; and the Egyptians pursued after your fathers with chariots and horsemen unto the Red sea.
>
> And when they cried unto the Lord, he put darkness between you and the Egyptians, and brought the sea upon them, and covered them; and your eyes have seen what I have done in Egypt: and ye dwelt in the wilderness a long season.
>
> And I brought you into the land of the Amorites, which dwelt on the other side Jordan; and they fought with you: and I gave them into your hand, that ye might possess their land; and I destroyed them from before you. . . .
>
> And ye went over Jordan, and came unto Jericho: and the men of Jericho fought against you, the Amorites, and the Perizzites, and the Canaanites, and the Hittites, and the Girgashites, the Hivites, and the Jebusites; and I delivered them into your hand. . . .
>
> And I have given you a land for which ye did not labour, and cities which ye built not, and ye dwell in them; of the vineyards and oliveyards which ye planted not do ye eat.

Now therefore fear the Lord, and serve him in sincerity and in truth: and put away the gods which your fathers served on the other side of the flood, and in Egypt; and serve ye the Lord. (Joshua 24:2–8, 11, 13–14.)

Once Israel was established in the land, the story of the Lord's deliverance not only became a part of their past story but became a living memory of God's mercy and love. Specifically, the Lord commanded the Israelites to repeat the Exodus story when they appeared before the Lord to offer the firstfruits of the land on the altar of the tabernacle: "A Syrian ready to perish was my father, and he went down into Egypt, and sojourned there with a few, and became there a nation, great, mighty, and populous: and the Egyptians evil entreated us, and afflicted us, and laid upon us hard bondage: and when we cried unto the Lord God of our fathers, the Lord heard our voice, and looked on our affliction, and our labour, and our oppression: and the Lord brought us forth out of Egypt with a mighty hand, and with an outstretched arm, and with great terribleness, and with signs, and with wonders: and he hath brought us into this place, and hath given us this land, even a land that floweth with milk and honey." (Deuteronomy 26:5–9.)

The story became etched in Israel's memory as a vivid reminder that the Lord was not only willing but able to deliver his covenant people. As the psalmist wrote:

O give thanks unto the Lord; call upon his name: make known his deeds among the people.

Sing unto him, sing psalms unto him: talk ye of all his wondrous works.

Glory ye in his holy name: let the heart of them rejoice that seek the Lord.

Seek the Lord, and his strength: seek his face evermore.

Remember his marvellous works that he hath done; his wonders, and the judgments of his mouth. . . .

He sent Moses his servant; and Aaron whom he had chosen.

They shewed his signs among them, and wonders in the land of Ham. . . .

He smote also all the firstborn in their land, the chief of all their strength.

He brought them forth also with silver and gold: and there was not one feeble person among their tribes.

Egypt was glad when they departed: for the fear of them fell upon them.

He spread a cloud for a covering; and fire to give light in the night. . . .

And he brought forth his people with joy, and his chosen with gladness:

And gave them the lands of the heathen: and they inherited the labour of the people;

That they might observe his statutes, and keep his laws. Praise ye the Lord. (Psalm 105:1–5, 26–27, 36–39, 43–45; see also Psalm 106.)

---

## Notes

1. See William J. Murname, "Egypt, History of (DYN 18–20)" *The Anchor Bible Dictionary,* 6 vols. (New York: Doubleday, 1992), 2:348–49; "Hyksos," Ibid., 3:346.

2. Information about Moses' life is found in both the Old and New Testaments; see Exodus 2:10–22 and Acts 7:23.

3. See S. Kent Brown, "Trust in the Lord: Exodus and Faith," in *The Old Testament and the Latter-day Saints* [Sperry Symposium 1986] (Salt Lake City: Randall Book Company, 1986), pp. 92–93.

4. Since the fourth century, Christian tradition has held Mount Sinai to be modern-day Gebel Musa ("Mountain of Moses"), a 7,363-foot peak situated in the mountain ranges of the Sinai peninsula's southern tip.

5. The equivalent phrases in the New Testament are found in 1 Peter 2:9.

# CHAPTER TWO

# A New Testament Parallel

Moses prophesied: "The Lord thy God will raise up unto thee a Prophet from the midst of thee, of thy brethren, like unto me; unto him ye shall hearken" (Deuteronomy 18:15). The New Testament writers testified on numerous occasions that Jesus of Nazareth fulfilled this prophecy, and later the Restoration added its witness (see Acts 3:22–26; JS—H 1:40).

The Gospels provide numerous examples of Jesus fulfilling Old Testament prophecies, and they also tie events from Jesus' life and ministry with the Exodus story. First, Jesus is portrayed as the great "I am" (John 8:58; Exodus 3:14). Second, as already noted, Jesus was saved from Herod's cruel edict, just as Moses was saved from Pharaoh's (see Matthew 2:16; Exodus 1:15–2:10). Third, Jesus is identified as the "Lamb of God," reminding us of the Passover lamb sacrificed as a substitute by the ancient Israelites (see John 1:29, 36). Fourth, Jesus is the living water, recalling the giving of water to the Israelites in the desert when Moses struck the rock (see John 4:6–14, 7:37–40; see also 1 Corinthians 10:4). Fifth, the brazen serpent is seen as a type and shadow of Christ being lifted up on the cross (see John 3:14–15; see also Numbers 21:4–9). Sixth, there is a similarity between Moses and Christ both being with God for forty days (Matthew 4:2; Luke 4:2; see also Exodus 24:18). Seventh, the reception of the

law at Mount Sinai and Jesus' sermon on the mount can be compared
(see Matthew 5). Eighth, Matthew reveals five distinct divisions in
Jesus' teaching, calling to mind the five books of Moses (see Matthew
5–7, 10, 13, 18, 24–25).[2] Ninth, Jesus' bread of life sermon reminds us
of the manna sent by God during Israel's wilderness wanderings (see
John 6:31–35, 48, 51; see also Exodus 16:15).[3] Tenth, Christ's experiences in the wilderness recall Israel's trials, testing, and suffering during the forty years in the desert (see Mark 1). Eleventh, Jesus' baptism
at Bethabara reminds us of Israel's entrance into the promised land
(see John 1:28). Twelfth, Jesus' death on the cross not only saved us
but consecrated us to God's service, just as the blood of the sacrificed
lamb consecrated the ancient Israelites (see John 17:19). Thirteenth,
Jesus feeding those that followed him into the wilderness with the
multiplication of fishes and loaves compares to the miracle of manna
(see John 6).[4] Fourteenth, Jesus' flight to and return from Egypt remind us of Israel's sojourn and exodus from the same land (see
Matthew 2:14–15). Fifteenth, Jesus' petition to "give us this day our
daily bread" (Matthew 6:11; see also Luke 11:3) recalls the command
in Exodus, "The people shall go out and gather a certain rate every
day" (Exodus 16:4).

The New Testament portrays Jesus' death as occurring at the time
of Passover. In particular, John indicates that Jesus died on the day before the special Sabbath passover, the Sabbath that fell at Passover.
According to John, the Passover meal was eaten on a Thursday
evening, linking the Last Supper with the Passover meal. Thus Jesus'
breaking of bread and blessing of wine during the special celebration
immortalized the significance of the Passover meal forever.

While the gospel writers see parallels between Israel's ancient exodus and the life and teachings of Jesus, they recognize that the mortal Messiah was not just another Moses but one who was greater than
Moses.

The parallel between the ancient exodus and the first-century spiritual exodus continues on the Day of Pentecost, fifty days following
Passover. The Holy Spirit descended on the leaders of the church, and

they immediately preached the good news about Jesus of Nazareth to a stunned audience. Luke's Acts narrative is filled with allusions to the Old Testament, especially the experience at Mount Sinai. Although Luke does not tell us where the followers of the risen Christ were assembled when the Spirit came, the subsequent scene seems to be in the temple court.

As with the Sinai experience, the Spirit's coming on the Day of Pentecost was attended by "a sound from heaven as of a rushing mighty wind" filling the house where they were gathered and was marked by the appearance of "tongues like as of fire." Then the followers "were all filled with the Holy Ghost, and began to speak with other tongues." (Acts 2:2–4.) Pentecost was not only an agricultural festival but also a celebration of the giving of the Torah on Sinai fifty days following the exodus from Egyptian bondage.

At Sinai, which is the symbolic representation of God's heavenly temple, the Israelites met him and received the law from him on tables made of stone. To prepare the people to receive his law and covenant, God commanded Moses to go to the people and "sanctify them to day and to morrow, and let them wash their clothes, and be ready against the third day: for the third day the Lord will come down in the sight of all the people upon mount Sinai" (Exodus 19:10–11). Here they became the people of God, "a kingdom of priests, and an holy nation" (Exodus 19:6). In the midst of lightnings, thunderings, and voices, the children of Israel covenanted to be the Lord's people (see Exodus 19:18–20).

Luke's allusion to the creation of the nation of Israel may be symbolic of what God had done through the new Passover—the sacrifice and atonement of Christ—the reception of the new law written "not in tables of stone, but in fleshy tables of the heart" (2 Corinthians 3:3), and the creation of new Israel—the Church—on this most joyous celebration.

As a result of their preaching in the temple court and the moving of the Holy Spirit among the Jews who had come to Jerusalem to celebrate this important festival (like the children of Israel coming to the mount in Exodus), about three thousand were baptized (see Acts 2:41). Of course, the covenant of baptism is similar to the covenant at Mount Sinai. The new people "continued stedfastly in the apostles' doctrine and fellowship, and in breaking of bread, and in prayers. And fear came upon every soul: and many wonders and signs were done by the apostles. And all that believed were together, and had all things common; and sold their possessions and goods, and parted them to all men, as every man had need. And they, continuing daily with one accord in the temple, and breaking bread from house to house, did eat their meat with gladness and singleness of heart, praising God, and having favour with all the people. And the Lord added to the church daily such as should be saved. (Acts 2:42–47.)

Paul also drew numerous parallels between the life, ministry, and death of Jesus and the Exodus story, as already noted several times. Additionally, he emphasized that the children of Israel's experiences were preserved as an example for us:

> Moreover, brethren, I would not that ye should be ignorant, how that all our fathers were under the cloud, and all passed through the sea;
>
> And were all baptized unto Moses in the cloud and in the sea;
>
> And did all eat the same spiritual meat;
>
> And did all drink the same spiritual drink: for they drank of that spiritual Rock that followed them: and that Rock was Christ.
>
> But with many of them God was not well pleased: for they were overthrown in the wilderness.
>
> Now these things were our examples, to the intent we should not lust after evil things, as they also lusted.
>
> Neither be ye idolaters, as were some of them; as it is written, The people sat down to eat and drink, and rose up to play.
>
> Neither let us commit fornication, as some of them committed, and fell in one day three and twenty thousand.
>
> Neither let us tempt Christ, as some of them also tempted, and were destroyed of serpents.

Neither murmur ye, as some of them also murmured, and were destroyed of the destroyer.

Now all these things happened unto them for ensamples: and they are written for our admonition, upon whom the ends of the world are come. (1 Corinthians 10:1–11.)

One of Paul's important contributions regarding the book of Exodus is his commentary found in the book of Hebrews. Specifically, Jesus is portrayed as the second Moses, the "mediator of the new covenant" (Hebrews 12:24). The author also shows that Jesus is the high priest of a new covenant (see Hebrews 8). The book of Hebrews outlines the symbolic relationship between the ancient tabernacle and its sacrifices and Jesus' life and ministry, particularly how Jesus was sacrificed once for all (see Hebrews 10).

The covenant made with new Israel and its parallel to the account in Exodus is also outlined in the writings of Peter. He states categorically that the Saints of God are "a chosen generation, a royal priesthood, an holy nation, a peculiar people" (1 Peter 2:9). This is an obvious allusion to the words of the Lord to Moses in Exodus 19; and as is the case with the book of Revelation, Peter has in mind something majestic. "And Moses went up unto God, and the Lord called unto him out of the mountain, saying, Thus shalt thou say to the house of Jacob, and tell the children of Israel; ye have seen what I did unto the Egyptians, and how I bare you on eagles' wings, and brought you unto myself. Now therefore, if ye will obey my voice indeed, and keep my covenant, then ye shall be a peculiar treasure unto me above all people: for all the earth is mine: and ye shall be unto me a kingdom of priests, and an holy nation. These are the words which thou shalt speak unto the children of Israel." (Exodus 19:3–6; see Revelation 1:6, 5:9–10.)

Peter understood the individual transforming power of Christ's atoning sacrifice in the lives of those who accepted him as Lord and Messiah (see, for example, Acts 2:37–40). Yet he articulates a much broader application of Old Testament doctrine. Peter wrote to the early Saints as the high priest might have written to the nation of Israel; the

Saints constituted a "nation" just as ancient Israel did. Indeed, the early Saints replaced covenant Israel as God's own people; and yet they were not a totally new society without a past. They were the continuation of God's work among the nations of the earth. They were chosen from among other nations as a special kind of kingdom, with the divine task of offering a unique priestly service to God.

Of course, all these ideas were present in the Old Testament that Peter and the Saints used during their ministry. The fundamental scriptural text for this vision was, of course, the material found in Exodus. Exodus 19 begins the most majestic section in the whole book of Exodus. The theme of this section is a consummate vision, playing a role of decisive importance in Israel's history and, in fact, in the history of humanity as a whole.

The children of Israel have been liberated by God's outstretched hand from Egyptian servitude. The scripture, as already noted, states in part: "Now therefore, if ye will obey my voice indeed, and keep my covenant, then ye shall be a peculiar treasure unto me above all people: for all the earth is mine: and ye shall be unto me a kingdom of priests, and an holy nation."

The conclusion of this passage is in reality a proposal: Israel should make a covenant and become a chosen people, a people of special possession, on condition that they accept certain obligations and responsibilities. All their firstborn were intended to be priests, not just the firstborn of the Levites. In the New Testament setting, Peter applied this kingdom theme to the new Christians, redeemed by Christ's blood.

The term *a peculiar people* in both the New Testament Greek and the Old Testament Hebrew does not mean strange and does not refer to some kind of dress and grooming code or an unusual set of beliefs. The word *peculiar* is the King James Version's equivalent to "purchased, preserved, special possession, or property."

Both ancient Israel and the New Testament Saints to whom Peter wrote were purchased by blood from slavery. As already noted, during the days of Pharaoh the children were in heavy bondage; and, through the slaying of the lamb as a substitution, they were passed over and liberated. In New Testament times, all humanity was in a state of bondage, spiritual or temporal. God's firstborn Son, the lamb of God, shed his own blood to purchase each person from death, hell, and Satan, thus allowing God to create a new nation that would serve him faithfully as their king.

Exodus 19 and 1 Peter 2 are, therefore, remarkable chapters in the Bible. In the first place, they discuss the creation of Israel as a social, political, and economic nation, separate from all other nations. The founding of a new nation-kingdom is a singular event. This remarkable event is even more transcendent than the mere emergence of a new country among the nations of the earth. Unlike that of other nations both in the Old and New Testament worlds, Israel's history did not begin with a mortal king; their king, their lawgiver, and their savior was God Almighty, not a human being.

The promise to those people standing at the foot of Mount Sinai and also to the Saints of the New Testament period could be paraphrased as follows: "Now, if you will obey me fully and keep my covenant, then out of all nations you will be my treasured possession, although the whole earth is mine. You will be for me a holy nation of kings and priests."

The covenant between God and Israel at Mount Sinai and in the New Testament is the outgrowth and extension of the Lord's covenant with Adam and Eve, Enoch, Noah, Abraham and Sarah, Isaac, and Jacob. It was renewed at Sinai and renewed again in the New Testament. Participation in the divine blessing is conditioned on obedience added to faith. To be a choice people can mean several things. First, to be a chosen people is to be a people belonging to God. Second, it is to choose God; anyone who chooses God is chosen.

To be a "kingdom of priests" is to constitute the Lord's kingdom, the people who acknowledge him as their king; and priests are to be wholly consecrated to his service. God's people, both individually and collectively, are to be set apart to do his will.

By audible consent, the people promised to obey the terms of the covenant. In Exodus we read: "And all the people answered together, and said, All that the Lord hath spoken we will do" (Exodus 19:8).

The parallel between Exodus and the New Testament shifts slightly since, paradoxically, the new nation was largely composed of men, women, and children who, being Gentiles, had long been regarded by the Jews as automatically disqualified from playing such a special role in history. Yet even this paradox could be illuminated in the Old Testament. Hosea, in his vivid representation of the infidelity of the chosen people, had talked of Israel's being called by God "not my people," and of the possibility that, when it repented, "not my people" would once more be called "my people" (see Hosea 1–2). The Gentiles, who had always seemingly been "not my people," were now through Christ's atonement a "chosen generation, a royal priesthood, an holy nation, a peculiar people" (1 Peter 2:9).

The application of the Exodus story is complete: bondage, redemption, and the establishment of a new kingdom, a "kingdom of priests." The New Testament Saints, therefore, "should shew forth the praises of him who hath called you out of darkness into his marvellous light: which in time past were not a people, but are now the people of God: which had not obtained mercy, but now have obtained mercy" (1 Peter 2:9–11).

In establishing the link between the Exodus story and its New Testament parallel, the book of Revelation is a fitting way to conclude our discussion. The New Testament ends with the awe-inspiring "Revelation of Jesus Christ" (Revelation 1:1) given to John on the Isle of Patmos.[5]

John introduces his revelation to the seven churches through a series of statements to remind them of their position, statements that John knew they would understand: "And from Jesus Christ, who is the faithful witness, and the first begotten of the dead, and the prince of the kings of the earth. Unto him that loved us, and washed us from our sins in his own blood, and hath made us kings and priests unto God and his Father; to him be glory and dominion for ever and ever. Amen." (Revelation 1:5–6.)

John is making an allusion to Exodus 19, like Peter did before him. John asserts that redemption through Jesus Christ involves liberation from bondage and slavery, which is the point of Exodus 19:6 as well.

In this context, John encourages the early Christian Saints to keep faith in the face of trial and persecution. It is Jesus as the lamb in ancient temple worship and symbolism that stands as the witness of God's covenant and promises, to which John will allude and which John hopes the Saints will recall as they experience the harsh realities of discipleship.

John expresses the dignity the Saints receive through the titles *basileia* (kingdom) and *hiereis* (priests), which were in ancient times the symbols of those who were bearers of political and sacral authority.[6] These words and other similar phrases found in Revelation may have been intended to be understood only by those who were initiated and familiar with their special meaning.

The purpose for ancient Israel's exodus from Egypt, as already noted, was similar to the "exodus" of the New Testament Saints from spiritual Egypt or Babylon: the sanctification of a people so the kingdom of God could be established on earth. During the Mosaic period, the formation of the kingdom of Israel was brought about by the intervention of God in history as the Lord stretched out his arm against the Egyptians and their gods. The children of Israel were brought into the wilderness on "eagles' wings" and came unto the Lord in his desert sanctuary (Exodus 19:4).

Anciently, the priests represented the people as they approached the Lord in the tabernacle and later in the temple at Jerusalem. The high priest wore two onyx stones on his shoulders bearing Israel's names, as well as a breastplate. The high priest also represented Christ. As with many symbols, there are often multiple applications. In this case, however, we want to emphasize the role of the priest as representing the children of Israel.

These priests were washed and anointed, wore "holy garments," and were set apart for their sacred duties (see Exodus 28–29). Allusions to the Mosaic tabernacle and the priestly clothing are abundant through-out the book of Revelation. Additionally, Revelation is full of images relating to the Exodus story in particular, such as John's portrayal of Jesus as the *new* Passover lamb in Revelation 5.

Central to the Passover feast was the sacrificial lamb "without blemish, a male of the first year" (Exodus 12:5). Twenty-nine of the thirty-four references to a lamb in the New Testament are found in Revelation, where Jesus is portrayed as a "Lamb as it had been slain" (Revelation 5:6). The lamb, as already noted earlier, is in effect a sub-stitute sacrifice. For John, the Lamb is worthy of praise because he was slain (see Revelation 5:9). The verb *sphazein* (to slaughter) refers to the violent death of the lamb and probably alludes to the slaughter-ing of the Passover lamb.[7] This image evokes the memory of ancient Israel's exodus and liberation from Egypt.

Additionally, the Lamb is worthy because he has purchased ("re-deemed" in the King James Version) a people for God from every tribe, tongue, people, and nation with his blood (see Revelation 5:9). The Lamb is pictured as a purchasing agent for God and has traveled throughout the whole earth to purchase a people for God. The price that is paid is his own blood. This metaphoric language is used to em-phasize the high value of the purchased ones as well as the infinite and eternal nature of Christ's atonement. The verb *agorazein* (to purchase or redeem) is a secular as well as a religious term.[8] It denotes a com-mercial transaction, as is also evident in Revelation 3:18 and 13:7. In this case, it probably refers to a slave market, reminiscent of Egypt's bondage and first-century slave culture, because people are the objects of the purchase. This is also true of the use of the word in Revelation 7, where 144,000 are purchased from every nation.

Finally, the Lamb is worthy because he "hast made us unto our God kings and priests" (Revelation 5:10). This phrase, "kings and priests," is another way of saying a "kingdom of priests." Thus John depicts redemption and salvation in economic language and political imagery and understands it as an event analogous to the liberation of Israel from the slavery of Egypt. The Lord commanded ancient Israel to establish the tabernacle among the people. Through the tabernacle and its ordinances, Israel could be made holy and consecrated to the Lord. Ancient Israel constituted the Lord's kingdom on earth, a people who acknowledged him as their king, and like the Levitical priests they were to be wholly consecrated to his service. As God's people both individually and collectively, they were set apart to do his will.

To become holy, consecrated, and set apart is the key theme of the "holiness code" of Leviticus, as noted earlier: "For I am the Lord that bringeth you up out of the land of Egypt, to be your God: ye shall therefore be holy, for I am holy" (Leviticus 11:45). Both as a new, holy nation and as individuals, Israel was to express holiness in every aspect of life, to the extent that all of life could have a certain sacred quality. Because of who the Lord is and what he has done, his people must dedicate themselves fully to him.

Just as ancient Israel eventually entered the promised land of Canaan, John informed the early Christians that they would enter the eternal promised land and reign on earth with Christ as the King and Lord over his people (see Revelation 19:16). The images of a *new* Israel, a *new* Exodus, a *new* tabernacle, a *new* Passover lamb, and a *new* Jerusalem are a major theme throughout the book.

---

## Notes

1. Additionally the comparison with Israel's forty years of wandering should be considered (see Exodus 16:35).

2. That this was a deliberate effort is revealed in the final words of each division: "And it came to pass, when Jesus had ended these sayings" (Matthew 7:28, for example).

3. For a similar application see Deuteronomy 8:3 and Jesus' quotation of it in Matthew 4:4.

4. Additional parallels may include Jesus' departure across the sea and the crowd's angry reaction or murmuring (see John 6:41–43).

5. For a detailed discussion see Richard Neitzel Holzapfel and David Rolph Seely, *My Father's House: Temple Worship and Symbolism in the New Testament* (Salt Lake City: Bookcraft, 1994), pp. 207–49.

6. See Elizabeth Schusster Fiorenza, *The Book of Revelation: Justice and Judgment* (Philadelphia: Fortress Press, 1985), p. 24.

7. See Max Zerwick and Mary Grosvenor, *A Grammatical Analysis of the Greek New Testament* (Rome: Biblical Institute Press, 1981), p. 750.

8. Walter Baeur, William F. Arhdt, and Wilbur F. Gingrich, ed., *A Greek-English Lexicon of the New Testament and Other Early Christian Literature* (Chicago: The University of Chicago Press, 1957), pp. 12–13.

CHAPTER THREE

# A Personal Parallel

*N*ephi said: "I did liken all scriptures unto us, that it might be for our profit and learning" (1 Nephi 19:23). The application of the Exodus story to our personal lives gives us a deeper appreciation of God's challenge: "Remember that thou wast a servant in the land of Egypt, and that the Lord thy God brought thee out thence through a mighty hand and by a stretched out arm" (Deuteronomy 5:15).

In one sense we have all been a "servant in the land of Egypt" at some time. However, the Lord's promise of ultimate deliverance from the trials, suffering, sins, and natural consequences of living in a fallen world will be fulfilled in our own lives, as was the promise made to Abraham about the ultimate delivery of his posterity from Egyptian bondage thousands of years ago.

In this way, the Exodus story has a personal application. Many of the events found in this remarkable biblical narrative are paralleled in the lives of each child of God who strives as Joshua proclaimed: "And if it seem evil unto you to serve the Lord, choose you this day whom ye will serve; whether the gods which your fathers served that were on the other side of the flood, or the gods of the Amorites, in whose land ye dwell: but as for me and my house, we will serve the Lord" (Joshua 24:15).

The focus of the Exodus story is on the lands stretching from the valley of the Nile in Egypt across the Sinai peninsula to Palestine. The Nile Valley is not only the central physical feature of Egypt but represents less than four percent of the land that was and is habitable. The rest is mostly desert, except for some areas along the seacoast. Sinai is a triangular land bridge joining Africa and Asia. The southern half rises steadily and is crossed by many wadis (Arabic for seasonal watercourse), which drain the land in the infrequent event of rain, and the topography culminates in mountain peaks. The highest of these is Gebel Musa (also known as Mountain of Moses or Mount Sinai). Beginning to the north of the Sinai peninsula and extending north as far as Syria, the land is divided roughly into a series of north-south strips: the coastal plains, a range of low hills, the main ridge of mountains, and the Jordan River Valley. Canaan, a land often referred to in scripture as Israel, is a narrow strip of land between the mountains east of the Jordan Valley and the sea. This region is called the Holy Land because of the events that took place there and because God's Son lived and died there.

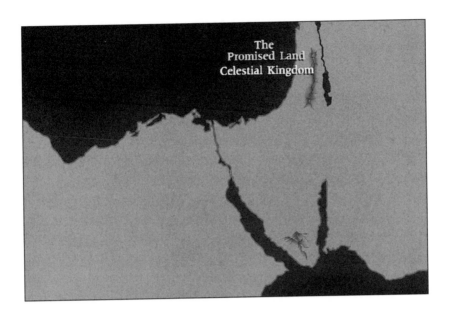

Canaan was the land promised to Abraham: "And I will give unto thee, and to thy seed after thee, the land wherein thou art a stranger, all the land of Canaan, for an everlasting possession" (Genesis 17:8). In a personal parallel, the promised land could represent the eternal inheritance of the faithful: the celestial kingdom. As part of the plan formulated and implemented eons ago, we lived in a pre-mortal existence as spirit sons and daughters of heavenly parents. In what is sometimes called the first estate, we lived with our heavenly parents but could progress and grow only to a certain point. In order to continue our progress and ultimately receive a fullness of joy, it was necessary to leave the presence of our heavenly parents and receive a physical body (see D&C 93:33–34). Before we came to earth we participated in the War in Heaven, where we chose to follow Jesus. The dissension among Jacob's sons before Joseph was sold into slavery may be a parallel to the conflict in heaven (see Genesis 37).

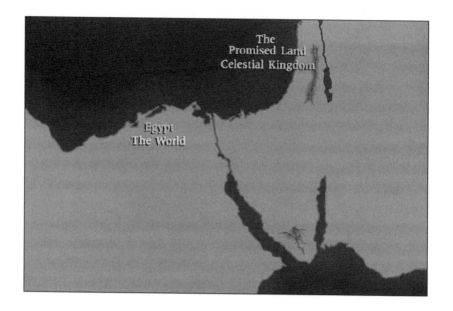

In this personal parallel, Egypt is a symbol of the world or of wickedness. Just as the children of Israel went into Egypt, we leave heaven and come to earth during a mortal probation. This mortal probation away from God's presence is a time of testing. In fact, an important part of the plan of redemption is that we need a place, an environment, where we can exercise our God-given right to act for ourselves. Only in utilizing our agency can we prove to ourselves and to the Lord our willingness to obey his commandments, as we learn in the book of Abraham (see Abraham 3:25).

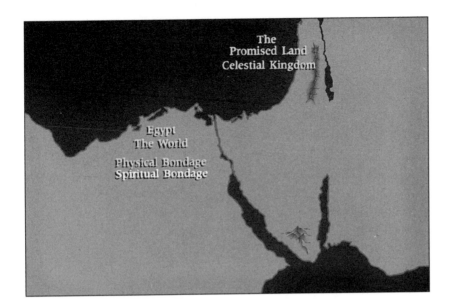

As the children of Israel dwelt in Egypt and became slaves of Pharaoh, so we experience mortality and become slaves to sin and to the effects of mortality, such as sickness, emotional struggles, and death. John preserved Jesus' profound statement made at the Last Supper: "In the world ye shall have tribulation" (John 16:33).

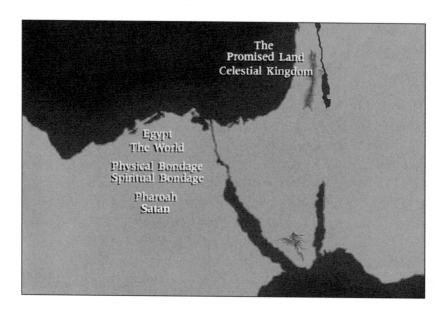

As the children of Israel served Pharaoh, so likewise do those held in bondage to sin serve Satan, who becomes the master of those enslaved by sin. The description of Israel's subjection by Egypt can remind us of the consequence of sin: "And they made their lives bitter with hard bondage . . . all their service, wherein they made them serve, was with rigour" (Exodus 1:14). Additionally, we all become subject to a mortal condition with passions, desires, and appetites as well as inevitable death. Jacob calls death "that awful monster" (2 Nephi 9:26).

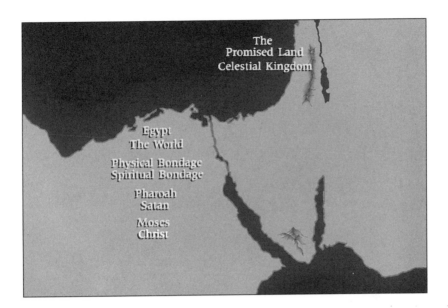

The
Promised Land
Celestial Kingdom

Egypt
The World

Physical Bondage
Spiritual Bondage

Pharoah
Satan

Moses
Christ

As the Lord sent a prophet to deliver the children of Israel, so God sent his Only Begotten Son as a deliverer. Jacob testifies: "O how great the goodness of our God, who prepareth a way for our escape from the grasp of this awful monster; yea, that monster, death and hell" (2 Nephi 9:10). Without Jesus Christ's atonement we could not be delivered from the consequences of sin and the natural effects of living in a mortal world. In this sense, Jesus is not only like Moses but he is also the firstborn sacrifice that finally allows the children of Israel to escape bitter bondage. While the death of the firstborn Egyptians may parallel the death of God's firstborn son, it is the passover lamb that acts as a substitute sacrifice which saves the firstborn Israelites from certain death when the angel passed over them on the terrible night of affliction.

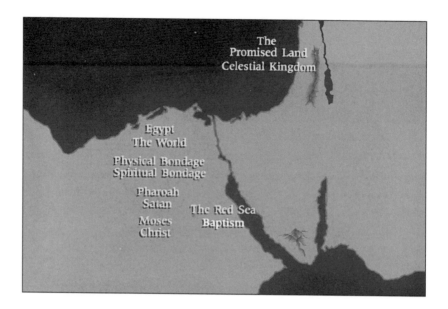

As the children of Israel made their escape from Egypt through the Red Sea, we escape the world symbolically through the waters of baptism: "Moreover, brethren, I would not that ye should be ignorant, how that all our fathers were under the cloud, and all passed through the sea; and were all baptized unto Moses in the cloud and in the sea" (1 Corinthians 10:1–2). Additionally, the "Red" could be analogous to the blood of the lamb which washes us from our sins: "Unto him that loved us, and washed us from our sins in his own blood" (Revelation 1:5).

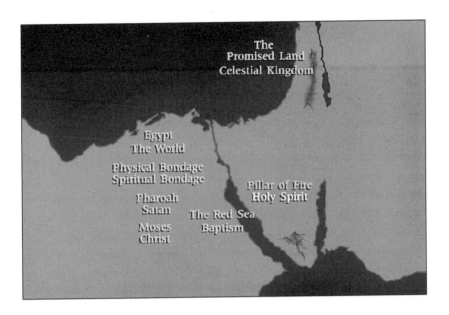

After their escape through the sea, the children of Israel were led in the wilderness by a pillar of fire and a cloud. These elements are not only symbolic of God's presence but for the modern Saint are representative of the promise of the father: the baptism of fire and the Holy Ghost received as a gift from God following baptism (see Matthew 3:11). The Holy Ghost is given as a comforter and a testifier but also as a guide leading us toward truth, as it says in scripture: "He will guide you into all truth" (John 16:13). Telestial existence into a terrestial existence spiritually prepares us to enter into the celestial kingdom. While in the wilderness the faithful are nourished with living water and with the bread of life, just as ancient Israel's thirst was relieved when Moses struck the rock and water gushed forth and just as the children of Israel received manna for bread from heaven (see John 4:6–14, 6:31–35).

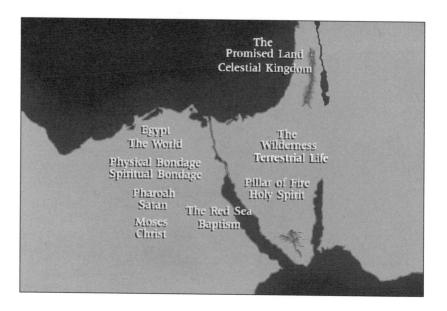

The pillar of fire and the cloud led the children of Israel to the mountain of God, where they made a covenant with him and received his law. We too are led by the Spirit to the temple to enter into eternal covenants and receive his law.

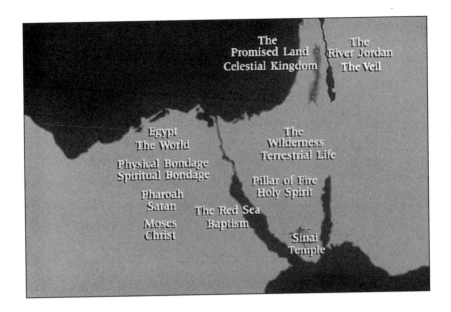

After escaping from Pharaoh's bondage in Egypt through the Red Sea and being led by a pillar of fire and a cloud to Mount Sinai to make a covenant with the Lord, the children of Israel eventually ended their wanderings in the wilderness and prepared to enter the Promised Land across Jordan, led by Joshua. As part of the great plan, God sent his Son to deliver us from the world and sin. As the children of Israel went through the Red Sea and followed the cloud and pillar to the mountain of God, we too pass through the waters of baptism and follow the Holy Spirit to the temple. Once we receive the sacred covenants revealed to the faithful, we then are prepared to cross the Jordan (the temple veil) into the eternal promised land after the days of our wandering are finished. At the end of our mortal probation (wilderness wandering), we follow a new Joshua (Joshua's name means "Yahweh [Jehovah] is Salvation"; the Greek form of the name Joshua is the same as that of the name Jesus):[1] "O then, my beloved brethren, come unto the Lord, the Holy One. Remember that his paths are righteous. Behold, the way for man is narrow, but it lieth in a straight course before him, and the keeper of the gate is the Holy One of Israel; and he employeth no servant there; and there is none other way save it be by the gate; for he cannot be deceived, for the Lord God is his name. And whoso knocketh, to him will he open." (2 Nephi 9:41–42.)

---

## Notes

1. See Ben F. Meyer, "Jesus Christ" *The Anchor Bible Dictionary* 6 Vols. (New York: Doubleday, 1992), 3:773.

# CHAPTER FOUR

# A Doctrine and Covenants Parallel

Since redemptive history is played out in the New Testament following a pattern from the Old Testament, one may expect a similar pattern to appear in the Restoration story. Or, at least, one could make an application to the earlier story in the history of The Church of Jesus Christ of Latter-day Saints.

Following the organization of the church of Christ on 6 April 1830, the Saints continued to be despised, harassed, and persecuted. It was only within a short time before Joseph Smith was commanded by the Lord: "Behold, I say unto you that it is not expedient in me that ye should translate any more until ye shall go to the Ohio, and this because of the enemy and for your sakes" (D&C 37:1).

In this Doctrine and Covenants parallel, New York represents Egypt. The call to Ohio is therefore a call to go into the wilderness of a modern Sinai. The Lord tells the Saints that they should leave New York "because of the enemy" and "for your sakes." What the Lord may have meant by the phrase "for your sakes" is possibly revealed in the next section of the Doctrine and Covenants: "Wherefore, for this cause I gave unto you the commandment that ye should go to the Ohio; and there I will give unto you my law; and there you shall be endowed with power from on high" (D&C 38:32).

This scripture is full of elements designed to recall Israel's reception of the law at Mount Sinai in the Old Testament and the endowment of power promised to the early apostles and fulfilled on the day of Pentecost in the New Testament, which as already noted is a direct parallel to the receiving of the law in Exodus.

It was only shortly after the Saints began to gather in Ohio that the Lord gave them the law recorded in Doctrine and Covenants 42: "Hearken, O ye elders of my church, who have assembled yourselves together in my name, even Jesus Christ the Son of the living God, the Savior of the world; inasmuch as ye believe on my name and keep my commandments. Again I say unto you, hearken and hear and obey the law which I shall give unto you." (D&C 42:1–2.)

The introduction to this section notes: "The Prophet specifies this revelation as 'embracing the law of the Church.'"

Contained in this particular revelation are many parallels to the Ten Commandments as found in the book of Exodus (see, for example, D&C 42:18–24). As the Saints gathered in Ohio (the wilderness in our analogy) they began to build a temple. Of course, temples have always represented mountains as places of holiness and sacredness.

Another parallel between the Exodus story and the Restoration is the connection between Moses' vision of the tabernacle before its construction and Joseph Smith's vision of the Kirtland Temple before its construction. "And let them make me a sanctuary," the Lord told Moses, "that I may dwell among them. According to all that I shew thee, after the pattern of the tabernacle, and the pattern of all the instruments thereof, even so shall ye make it." (Exodus 25:8–9.) To Joseph the Lord said, "Now here is wisdom, and the mind of the Lord—let the house be built, not after the manner of the world, for I give not unto you that ye shall live after the manner of the world; therefore, let it be built after the manner which I shall show unto three of you, whom ye shall appoint and ordain unto this power." (D&C 95:13–14).

Later, Joseph Smith, Sidney Rigdon, and Frederick G. Williams, members of the Presidency of the High Priesthood (or First Presidency), saw the temple in vision. Brigham Young tied this event to the Exodus story when he said: "Joseph not only received revelation and commandment to build a Temple, but he received a pattern also, as did Moses for the Tabernacle, . . . for without a pattern, he could not know what was wanting, having never seen one, and not having experienced its use."[1]

Shortly after the law of the Church was given, another revelation contained these words: "Again I say, hearken ye elders of my church, whom I have appointed: Ye are not sent forth to be taught, but to teach the children of men the things which I have put into your hands by the power of my Spirit; and ye are to be taught from on high. Sanctify yourselves and ye shall be endowed with power, that ye may give even as I have spoken." (D&C 43:15–16.)

The command to sanctify reminds us of the call in Exodus: "And the Lord said unto Moses, Go unto the people, and sanctify them to day and to morrow, and let them wash their clothes, and be ready against the third day: for the third day the Lord will come down in the sight of all the people upon mount Sinai" (Exodus 19:10–11). The promise of an endowment, again, relates to Jesus' command to the ancient disciples: "And, behold, I send the promise of my Father upon you: but tarry ye in the city of Jerusalem, until ye be endued with power from on high" (Luke 24:49).

The temple context of both is seen in a comment by the Prophet Joseph Smith: "At one time God obtained a house where Peter was[hed] and ano[inte]d &c on the day of pentecost."[2]

It is certain that in the Restoration parallel, two sites represent the promised land. First, the land of Missouri: "And thus, even as I have said, if ye are faithful ye shall assemble yourselves together to rejoice upon the land of Missouri, which is the land of your inheritance" (D&C 52:42).[3] Second, the Great Basin, where the Saints settled more than seven hundred settlements during the nineteenth century. For our purposes, we will utilize the latter as the type of the promised land.

Back in Ohio, the Saints continued in their effort to build the first temple in the last dispensation. A few days after Christmas 1837, the

Lord reminded the Saints: "Therefore, sanctify yourselves that your minds become single to God, and the days will come that you shall see him; for he will unveil his face unto you, and it shall be in his own time, and in his own way, and according to his own will. Remember the great and last promise which I have made unto you." (D&C 88:68–69.)

Again, the Lord uses language meant to help us recall earlier events: "Tarry ye, tarry ye in this place" (D&C 88:70) is similar to the Lord's command to the early disciples, "Tarry ye in the city of Jerusalem" (Luke 24:49). The Lord further explained to the disciples in Kirtland: "And I give unto you, who are the first laborers in this last kingdom, a commandment that you assemble yourselves together, and organize yourselves, and prepare yourselves, and sanctify yourselves; yea, purify your hearts, and cleanse your hands and your feet before me, that I may make you clean" (D&C 88:74).

Additionally, the Lord says: "Organize yourselves; prepare every needful thing; and establish a house, even a house of prayer, a house of fasting, a house of faith, a house of learning, a house of glory, a house of order, a house of God" (D&C 88:119).

Sometime in 1833, the Lord made another connection to the ancient story more clearly than almost any other reference in the Doctrine and Covenants: "Yea, verily I say unto you, I gave unto you a commandment that you should build a house, in the which house I design to endow those whom I have chosen with power from on high; for this is the promise of the Father unto you; therefore I command you to tarry, even as mine apostles at Jerusalem" (D&C 95:8–9).

In both the Kirtland and Jerusalem experiences, one of the purposes was to prepare the disciples to "go into all the world to preach [the] gospel" (D&C 18:28; see also Matthew 28:18–19; Luke 24:47).

Again, the parallel expands as the pentecostal outpouring manifests itself over a longer period of time during the Restoration drama. Beginning on January 27, 1836, and continuing through the summer, the pentecostal period of the Church is well documented. Marvelous blessings came on the evening of January 21, 1836, after Joseph Smith and some brethren instituted the first washings and anointings in this dispensation: "The heavens were opened upon us, and I beheld the celestial kingdom of God, and the glory thereof, whether in the body or out I cannot tell. I saw the transcendent beauty of the gate through which the heirs of that kingdom will enter, which was like unto circling flames of fire; also the blazing throne of God, whereon was seated the Father and the Son." (D&C 137:1–3.)

Soon the Saints finished the temple and the dedication service was ready. During the service on March 27, 1836, Joseph Smith offered a prayer of dedication. Among the many specific blessings he asked for was one particular request: "Let the anointing of thy ministers be sealed upon them with power from on high. Let it be fulfilled upon them, as upon those on the day of Pentecost; let the gift of tongues be poured out upon thy people, even cloven tongues as of fire, and the interpretation thereof. And let thy house be filled, as with a rushing mighty wind, with thy glory." (D&C 109:35–37.)

As evening Passover celebrations began in Jerusalem, Joseph Smith and Oliver Cowdery found themselves in the recently dedicated temple in Kirtland. During the Sabbath day meeting the Prophet Joseph Smith "retired to the pulpit, the veils being dropped, and bowed myself, with Oliver Cowdery, in solemn and silent prayer. After rising from prayer, the following vision was opened to both of us." (D&C 110, introduction.) The visions manifested to Joseph Smith and Oliver Cowdery connected the Kirtland Temple to the Exodus story in several meaningful ways. First, the Lord appeared to them as he appeared to Moses (see D&C 110:1–10), recalling the appearance of the Lord at Mount Sinai: "Then went up Moses, and Aaron, Nadab, and Abihu, and seventy of the elders of Israel: and they saw the God of Israel: and there was under his feet as it were a paved work of a sapphire stone, and as it were the body of heaven in his clearness" (Exodus 24:9).

Second, the scripture records: "After this vision closed, the heavens were again opened unto us; and Moses appeared before us, and committed unto us the keys of the gathering of Israel from the four parts of the earth, and the leading of the ten tribes from the land of the north" (D&C 110:11). The dedication and the manifestations at the Kirtland Temple constitute one of the great aspects of the Restoration story.

Another parallel between the Exodus story and the Restoration may be the rebellion and judgment which occurred in Kirtland following the pentecostal period. Like the rebellion of the children of Israel when they made a golden calf as described in Exodus 32, many of the Saints were involved in "speculation and wickedness." As the Church newspaper noted, they were "guilty of wild speculation and visionary dreams of wealth and worldly grandeur, as if gold and silver were their gods, and houses, farms and merchandize their only bliss or their passport to it."[4] While in the Exodus story three thousand rebels were slain, in the Restoration parallel many died spiritually during this period of rebellion and judgment.

Throughout the Doctrine and Covenants, the Lord reminds the Saints: "Listen to him who is the advocate with the Father, who is pleading your cause before him—saying: Father, behold the sufferings and death of him who did no sin, in whom thou wast well pleased; behold the blood of thy Son which was shed, the blood of him whom thou gavest that thyself might be glorified; wherefore, Father, spare these my brethren that believe on my name, that they may come unto me and have everlasting life" (D&C 45:3–5). This recalls Moses' efforts to act as a mediator between the people and the Lord: "And Moses besought the Lord his God, and said, Lord, why doth thy wrath wax hot against thy people, which thou hast brought forth out of the land of Egypt with great power, and with a mighty hand? . . . Remember Abraham, Isaac, and Israel, thy servants, to whom thou swarest by thine own self, and saidst unto them, I will multiply your seed as the stars of heaven, and all this land that I have spoken of will I give unto your seed, and they shall inherit it for ever." (Exodus 32:11, 13.)

Similar to the experiences the Israelites had in their wanderings, in time the Saints gathered in Missouri and Illinois only to be driven by persecution to find their land of promise in the west.

When the Saints decided to leave Nauvoo, the movement became known as the "Exodus to Greatness." Many people then saw parallels between their movement and that of the children of Israel.[5] The crossing of the Mississippi was analogous to the crossing of the Red Sea. The river freezing was likened to the parting of the Red Sea. Additionally, when the poor Saints were able to gather quails which had landed in their midst, it was seen as a miracle similar to the sending of manna from heaven.

Finding themselves on the western border of the United States on the Missouri River, they prepared to begin a trek to the Great Basin. On January 14, 1847, Brigham Young received the "Word and Will of the Lord" (D&C 136:1). In this revelation, the Lord again drew a comparison between the modern Saints and the ancient Israelites: "The Word and Will of the Lord concerning the Camp of Israel in their journeyings to the West" (D&C 136:1). Additionally, the revelation utilized language similar to the book of Exodus, including the words *covenant, commandments, statutes,* and *ordinances* (see D&C 136:2, 4). Also, the organization of the camp with "captains of hundreds, captains of fifties, and captains of tens" (D&C 136:3) reminded the Saints of a passage in Exodus: "Moreover thou shalt provide out of all the people able men, such as fear God, men of truth, hating covetousness; and place such over them, to be rulers of thousands, and rulers of hundreds, rulers of fifties, and rulers of tens" (Exodus 18:21).

Again, the revelation echoes with the language of Exodus: "I am the Lord your God, even the God of your fathers, the God of Abraham and of Isaac and of Jacob" (D&C 136:21). And more explicitly the Lord refers to himself: "I am he who led the children of Israel out of the land of Egypt; and my arm is stretched out in the last days, to save my people Israel" (D&C 136:22). Other passages in this revelation find parallels in Exodus and Deuteronomy (see, for example, D&C 136:26, 30, 40).

When some of the Saints questioned the deaths of Joseph and Hyrum, the Lord reminded them: "Have I not delivered you from your enemies, only in that I have left a witness of my name?" (D&C 136:40.) The combination of the phrases "Camp of Israel" and "Have I not delivered you" reinforced the Saints' idea that they were in fact reenacting the exodus of ancient Israel from Egypt to the Promised Land. Brigham Young became the "American Moses" who led his people to a promised land in the Great Basin.

The most interesting aspect of this process is the analogue between the three features in the Holy Land and three features in Utah: the Dead Sea and the Great Salt Lake, the River Jordan (Israel) and the Jordan River (Utah), and the Sea of Galilee and Utah Lake. While many dissimilarities exist between the two regions—elevation and climate, for instance—there are many similarities: first, the salt content in both the Dead Sea and Great Salt Lake; second, the fresh water intake of both from a fresh-water lake; third, both rivers connecting the salt lakes function in similar ways; and finally, both Galilee and Utah Lake were important fisheries. The drama is further played out when other biblical names were used to create a sense of the holiness of the newfound Zion, such as Salem (a town), Israel and Enoch (canyons), Ensign and Mount Nebo (prominent peaks), and Jacob's Ladder (a group of hilltops).

Wilford Woodruff noted in his journal on the day he arrived in the Salt Lake Valley with Brigham Young that it was "a land of promise, held in reserve by the hand of God for a resting place of the Saints."[6]

Heber C. Kimball addressed the importance of properly honoring the Promised Land. "If you wish to go hunting, fishing, or to see the country, select a week day and not the Lord's day for that purpose. Do not let us get giddy and light minded as the Nephites did of old, but strive to work righteousness in the beginning, inasmuch as we have reached the promised land."[7]

Once settled in the Promised Land, the Latter-day Saints sought to establish a "kingdom of priests, and an holy nation" (Exodus 19:6). Only four days after Brigham Young completed the 1847 trek to the Salt Lake Valley, he walked to a spot between two creeks, waved his hand, and said, "Here is the [ten] acres for the temple."[8] In April 1853

President Young recalled the visionary experience he had at the site: "I scarcely ever say much about revelations, or visions, but suffice it to say, five years ago last July [1847] I was here, and saw in the Spirit the Temple not ten feet from where we have laid the Chief Corner Stone. I have not inquired what kind of a Temple we should build. Why? Because it was represented before me. I have never looked upon that ground, but the vision of it was there. I see it as plainly as if it was in reality before me. Wait until it is done. I will say, however, that it will have six towers."[9]

Certainly, there is a parallel between this event and the building of the temple in Jerusalem by the Israelites. Just as Moses had seen a pattern of the tabernacle at Sinai, so Joseph Smith had seen the pattern of the temple in Kirtland. As Solomon built a permanent temple in the promised land, so Brigham Young did the same. We quoted earlier from Brigham Young regarding the vision Joseph had before the Kirtland Temple was built: "Joseph not only received revelation and commandment to build a Temple, but he received a pattern also, as did Moses for the Tabernacle, *and Solomon for his Temple;* for without a pattern, he could not know what was wanting, having never seen one, and not having experienced its use."[10] Apparently, the patterns of both holy structures came as a result of a vision, just as the patterns for the Kirtland and Salt Lake Temples came to the leaders of modern Israel.

Not only was the temple design part of a revelation and vision, but the Salt Lake Temple was located in the heart of the new settlement and the ancient tabernacle was found in the heart of the Israelite camp as they wandered in the wilderness.

Creating a sense of holiness in the new promised land, the Saints utilized powerful and emotionally laden symbols, such as the all-seeing eye, crowns, the handclasp of fellowship, and the phrase, "Holiness to the Lord," reminding them of the covenant relationship between themselves and God and reflecting two Old Testament scripture passages: "And thou shalt make a plate of pure gold, and grave upon it, like the engravings of a signet, HOLINESS TO THE LORD. And thou shalt put it on a blue lace, that it may be upon the mitre; upon the forefront of the mitre it shall be. And it shall be upon Aaron's forehead." (Exodus 28:36–38.) "In that day shall there be upon the bells of the horses, HOLINESS UNTO THE LORD; and the pots in the Lord's house shall be like the bowls before the altar. Yea, every pot in Jerusalem and in Judah shall be holiness unto the Lord of hosts." (Zechariah 14:20–21.)

The story of the Restoration and the Church's early history is a magnificent one, independent of any parallels to the past. Yet these parallels between the modern dispensation and past dispensations can help us appreciate the promises of deliverance. Whether as individuals or as a people collectively, we know that "the tender mercies of the Lord are over all those whom he hath chosen, because of their faith, to make them mighty even unto the power of deliverance." (1 Nephi 1:20).

---

## Notes

1. In *Journal of Discourses,* 2:31.

2. Joseph Smith Diary, 11 June 1843, Joseph Smith Papers, Historical Department, The Church of Jesus Christ of Latter-day Saints, Salt Lake City.

3. In a revelation given to Joseph Smith in 1834, the Lord provides this parallel: "Behold, I say unto you, the redemption of Zion must needs come by power; Therefore, I will raise up unto my people a man, who shall lead them like as Moses led the children of Israel. For ye are the children of Israel, and of the seed of Abraham, and ye must needs be led out of bondage by power, and with a stretched-out arm. And as your fathers were led at the first, even so shall the redemption of Zion be. Therefore, let not your hearts faint, for I say not unto you as I said unto your fathers: Mine angel shall go up before you, but not my presence. But I say unto you: Mine angels shall go up before you, and also my presence, and in time ye shall possess the goodly land." (D&C 103:15–20.) Apparently, the concrete historical context suggest that this prophecy specifically refers to the Prophet Joseph Smith (Moses

type) and the redemption of Zion (Missouri or the Promised Land). In "likening scripture" we could say that at another time and place, Brigham Young acted as Moses and helped the Saints gain a "goodly land"; see D&C 136:1, 21–22.

4. *Messenger and Advocate,* May 1837, p. 509.

5. Susan Easton Black recently spoke on this subject and noted many parallels; see Susan Easton Black, *Brigham Young, The American Moses* (unpublished manuscript in author's possession.)

6. Journal of Wilford Woodruff, 24 July 1847, LDSCA.

7. Heber C. Kimball discourse of 25 July 1847; as cited in *William Clayton's Journal* [Salt Lake City: Clayton Family Association, 1921], p. 316.

8. Journal of Wilford Woodruff, 27 July 1847, LDSCA.

9. In *Journal of Discourses,* 1:133.

10. In *Journal of Discourses* 2:31; emphasis added.

# Conclusion

$\mathcal{T}$he story of God's power to deliver his people is one of the key themes in ancient and modern scripture, whether referring to temporal or spiritual difficulties. Often the scriptures refer to the Lord as the Redeemer when speaking of this deliverance. Of the many passages, none is better known than Job's declaration in the Old Testament: "For I know that my redeemer liveth, and that he shall stand at the latter day upon the earth" (Job 19:25). To fully appreciate the nuances of this bold declaration, a brief review of the biblical background of the use of the term *redeemer* is helpful.

God's relationship with Israel is often depicted as analogous to that of king to subject, of father to son, of husband to wife, and, more importantly for our discussion, as redeemer to redeemed. The doctrinal dimension of these relationships is based upon a social and legal foundation. In this context, redemption usually refers to the rescue of a person from an obligation by the means of a monetary payment.

According to the book of Leviticus, physical property, such as land and houses, could be reclaimed through monetary payment. As stewards of God's creation and tenants on God's land, the Israelites were given the land with the right to utilize its resources to sustain life and erect a temple to the Lord. If an impoverished Israelite sold his land to raise cash, a kinsman was supposed to redeem it. If he could not, the land would automatically return to the impoverished original tenant or to his heirs at the jubilee. (See Leviticus 25:8–23.)

In another setting, if an impoverished Israelite sold himself into indentured servitude, he had the same right of redemption that existed with relationship to land. Indentured servitude was not slavery since Israelites could not serve in perpetuity because they were ultimately God's servants who he had removed from Egypt (see Leviticus 25:55).

As a token of remembrance of the tenth plague, all firstborn were sanctified and subject to being sacrificed to God (see Exodus 13:15). However, under prescribed circumstances substitutions could be made. At the age of one month, all firstborn male Israelites were to be redeemed by five shekels (see Exodus 13:15–16; Numbers 3:46–51).

Another case included the redemption of a daughter sold as a maidservant. The story of Ruth fits well in this situation. When Boaz called Ruth "my daughter," he may have been saying, "I am adopting you as my daughter, and I will redeem you as one redeems his daughter from servitude." (See Exodus 21:7–8; Ruth 3:10.)

According to Leviticus, the obligation of redeeming devolved upon the nearest relative (see Leviticus 25:48–49). The *gō'ēl* (redeemer), therefore, was responsible for the well-being of his kin; he had the right and the ability of redemption. Apparently, the redeemer held a special position of honor to the one redeemed as long as he lived. Once the redeemer died, that obligation disappeared, and the one redeemed came fully back into the family as if he or she had never been in bondage.

In this light, Job's declaration "For I know that my redeemer liveth" (Job 19:25) may refer to an eternal obligation Job, the redeemed one, felt toward the Lord his redeemer. Like Job, other prophets taught that the Lord is the ultimate redeemer-rescuer of his children and his people from adversity. In one case, the Lord is introduced as the one "who redeemed Abraham" (Isaiah 29:22).

As already noted, the archetypal act of divine redemption was the Lord's saving Israel from bondage in Egypt. In Exodus, God redeemed the Israelites from the suffering of Egypt and saved them from slavery in order to make them his people (see Exodus 6:6–7). Eventually, he brought them to the promised land, a fulfillment of the promise he made to Abraham. In the Song of the Sea, the redeemed people are led to God's pasture (see Exodus 15:13).

The Lord redeemed Israel from distress and bondage, and the scriptural record testifies that the Lord will continue to redeem individuals and the collective body of believers from present distress and from future exile at the end of time. One thing is certain: the Lord has continually sought to remind us that redemption is possible through faith on his name.

> Wherefore, redemption cometh in and through the Holy Messiah; for he is full of grace and truth.
>
> Behold, he offereth himself a sacrifice for sin, to answer the ends of the law, unto all those who have a broken heart and a contrite spirit; and unto none else can the ends of the law be answered.
>
> Wherefore, how great the importance to make these things known unto the inhabitants of the earth, that they may know that there is no flesh that can dwell in the presence of God, save it be through the merits, and mercy, and grace of the Holy Messiah, who layeth down his life according to the flesh, and taketh it again by the power of the Spirit. . . .
>
> Wherefore, he is the firstfruits unto God, inasmuch as he shall make intercession for all the children of men; and they that believe in him shall be saved. (2 Nephi 2:6–9.)

The Exodus story is one of the most vivid and dramatic reminders of the Lord's redemption "through a mighty hand and by a stretched out arm" (Deuteronomy 5:15). While we certainly should remember this particular story, it is the experience, as Nephi tells us, of being "encircled about eternally in the arms of his love" (2 Nephi 1:15) which gives us personal assurance of the divine promises of the Lord.

Having been tried and tested by the Lord during our long travels and wanderings, we come to trust the Lord and learn to completely rely upon his stretched out arm and mighty hand for all our wants and needs and ultimately for our deliverance from the awful monsters of devil, and death, and hell, as discussed by the great Book of Mormon prophet Jacob (see 2 Nephi 9:13).

# *Index*